Redux Made Easy with Rematch

Reduce Redux boilerplate and apply best practices with Rematch

Sergio Moreno

REMATCH IS AN IMPRINT OF PACKT PUBLISHING

Redux Made Easy with Rematch

Copyright © 2021 Packt Publishing

Associate Group Product Manager: Pavan Ramchandani

Publishing Product Manager: Aaron Tanna

Senior Editor: Hayden Edwards

Content Development Editor: Feza Shaikh

Technical Editor: Shubham Sharma

Copy Editor: Safis Editing

Project Coordinator: Manthan Patel

Proofreader: Safis Editing

Indexer: Sejal Dsilva

Production Designer: Nilesh Mohite

First published: August 2021

Production reference: 1270821

Published by Packt Publishing Ltd.

Livery Place

35 Livery Street

Birmingham

B3 2PB, UK.

978-1-80107-621-0

www.packt.com

Contributors

About the author

Sergio Moreno is a frontend developer with more than 4 years of experience heavily focused on the analysis, design, development, and building of large-scale applications. Formerly working at Allfunds, the world's largest fund distribution network, he led the frontend team to build a full new suite of products for the new digital section of Allfunds. He entered the open source world in 2019 and has contributed to big companies including Google, Facebook, Airbnb, Pinterest, and many more. In 2020, he focused on contributions to Rematch, where he released the v2 version with a full rewrite of the code base, full compatibility with TypeScript, and many other improvements, such as reducing the bundle size in some cases by 80%. He is also now the lead mantainer of the LinguiJS library, an amazing internationalization library. He helped to release the v3 version and took on the role of leading the coming years of development of LinguiJS.

In 2021, he joined Flowable as a product engineer, working on their compact and highly efficient workflow and business process management platform for developers, system admins, and business users.

I would like to say a big thank you to everyone involved in the release of this book – for me, it has been such an amazing experience that I'll never forget. Thanks to everyone who has contributed to making this possible – Shawn and Blair, the creators of Rematch, and the amazing open source community around Rematch and Redux, thank you all.

About the reviewers

Mark Erikson is a software engineer living in southwest Ohio, USA. Mark is a Redux maintainer, creator of Redux Toolkit, and general keeper of the Redux docs. He tweets at acemarke, and frequently blogs about React, Redux, and other web dev topics. He spends much of his time answering questions about React and Redux anywhere there's a comment box on the internet, and usually hangs out in the Reactiflux chat channels.

Zhi Tian is a frontend developer living in Beijing, China. Zhi is working at Kuaishou, the China's second-largest short video company, he focused mainly on enterprise software development and SaaS. He is a software engineering graduate from Harbin Institute of Technology, one of the top global universities in engineering. He is an active contributor of open source community and an enthusiast of TypeScript and the type system behind it. As a collaborator of Rematch he has contributed a lot, especially the improvement of the Rematch type system.

Table of Contents

7

Introducing Testing to Rematch

8

The Rematch Plugins Ecosystem

Section 3: Diving Deeper into Rematch

9

Composable Plugins – Create Your First Plugin

10

Rewrite a Full Code Base from JavaScript to TypeScript

11

Rematch with React Native and Expo – A Real-World Mobile App

12

Rematch Performance Improvements and Best Practices

13

Conclusion

Other Books You May Enjoy

Index

Preface

Rematch is Redux best practices without the boilerplate. This book is an easy-to-read guide for anyone who wants to get started with Redux, and for those who are already using it and want to improve their code base.

Complete with hands-on tutorials, projects, and self-assessment questions, this easy-to-follow guide will take you from the simplest through to the most complex layer of Rematch. You'll learn how to migrate from Vanilla Redux to Rematch, even from JavaScript to Typescript. You'll also learn how to create Rematch plugins from scratch and how they can be used in any Rematch application. You'll then build a real-world application from the first steps, doing the design and preparing the layout, to later, with the power of Rematch and its plugins, building a superpowerful shopping application. As you advance, you'll see how plugins extend Rematch functionalities, understanding how they work and how they can be used in our Rematch applications. You'll learn how to do everything you need to build a React website and React Native application from the first steps of designing the interface to later ones such as publishing, testing, and optimizing performance.

Finally, we'll analyze the future of Rematch and how the frontend ecosystem is becoming easier to use and maintain with alternatives to Redux.

By the end of this book, you'll be able to have total control of the application state and use Rematch to manage its scalability with simplicity.

Who this book is for

This book is for React and Redux developers looking for better alternatives to Redux. Familiarity with JavaScript, React, and Redux will help you make the most of this book.

What this book covers

Chapter 1, Why Redux? An Introduction to Redux Architecture, analyzes in depth what design limitations Redux was designed to fix and how it evolved to be the framework that it is today.

Chapter 2, Why Rematch over Redux? An Introduction to Rematch Architecture, briefly explores Rematch's most basic concepts to get started and why and how it was created.

Chapter 3, Redux First Steps – Creating a Simple To-Do App, looks at creating a simple to-do tasks website using Vanilla JavaScript and Redux.

Chapter 4, From Redux to Rematch – Migrating a To-Do App to Rematch, covers migrating the previous to-do tasks website to Rematch, looking at the biggest differences.

Chapter 5, React with Rematch – The Best Couple – Part I, demonstrates, step by step, how to create a shopping store with the latest React technologies, such as Hooks, and using the most modern frameworks, such as Tailwind CSS, and bundling it with Vite.

Chapter 6, React with Rematch – The Best Couple – Part II, looks at how to introduce business logic with Rematch and binding this logic into reusable React components.

Chapter 7, Introducing Testing to Rematch, explains how to set up a real testing suite step by step, testing the business logic and the user interface with the latest frameworks, such as Jest and React Testing Library.

Chapter 8, The Rematch Plugins Ecosystem, explores how Rematch Plugins easily extend Rematch functionality through the official API, analyzing in depth how they work internally and explaining the most important concepts.

Chapter 9, Composable Plugins – Create Your First Plugin, runs through creating a Rematch plugin ready to be published and used by everyone on the ground.

Chapter 10, Rewrite a Full Code Base from JavaScript to TypeScript, goes through migrating our shopping store website to TypeScript, focusing a lot on which types Rematch exports and how these utility types can warn us about possible bugs in our business logic.

Chapter 11, Rematch with React Native and Expo – A Real-World Mobile App, goes through setting up a monorepo architecture from scratch, where we'll learn how Rematch makes it extremely easy to share business logic with the entire organization and how this logic can be reused in other frameworks like React Native.

Chapter 12, Rematch Performance Improvements and Best Practices, analyzes which optimizations can be done to our shopping store website and we'll learn how we can measure our website performance before applying any optimization.

Chapter 13, Conclusion, discusses the future of Rematch and how the frontend ecosystem, and especially state management solutions, have become more user-friendly lately, and what alternatives to Rematch exist today.

To get the most out of this book

You will need a version of Node.js equal to or higher than 12 (LTS recommended). All code examples have been tested locally with Node.js 14 and above on macOS Big Sur and later, but they should work with future versions and other operating systems. The Rematch version used in the book is greater than or equal to version 2.

Software/hardware covered in the book	Operating system requirements
Node.js LTS	macOS, Linux, or Windows
Yarn 1.22	macOS, Linux, or Windows
Google Chrome	macOS, Linux, or Windows
Visual Studio Code	macOS, Linux, or Windows

If you are using the digital version of this book, we advise you to type the code yourself or access the code from the book's GitHub repository (a link is available in the next section). Doing so will help you avoid any potential errors related to the copying and pasting of code.

After reading the book, I encourage you to visit `https://rematchjs.org` and join the official Discord Rematch Community (`https://discord.gg/zMzsMGvEHk`) where we answer any questions and we try to solve any problems you find with Rematch.

Download the example code files

You can download the example code files for this book from GitHub at `https://github.com/PacktPublishing/Redux-Made-Easy-with-Rematch`. If there's an update to the code, it will be updated in the GitHub repository.

We also have other code bundles from our rich catalog of books and videos available at `https://github.com/PacktPublishing/`. Check them out!

Download the color images

We also provide a PDF file that has color images of the screenshots and diagrams used in this book. You can download it here:

`https://static.packt-cdn.com/downloads/9781801076210_ColorImages.pdf`.

Conventions used

There are a number of text conventions used throughout this book.

`Code in text`: Indicates code words in text, database table names, folder names, filenames, file extensions, pathnames, dummy URLs, user input, and Twitter handles. Here is an example: "Rematch models contain a `state` property, a `reducers` property, and an `effects` property."

A block of code is set as follows:

```
const value = 10_000
console.log(value.toLowerCase())
```

When we wish to draw your attention to a particular part of a code block, the relevant lines or items are set in bold:

```
export const shop = createModel<RootModel>()({
  state: {},
  reducers: {},
  effects: (dispatch) => ({})
})
```

Any command-line input or output is written as follows:

```
yarn add --dev typescript
```

Bold: Indicates a new term, an important word, or words that you see onscreen. For instance, words in menus or dialog boxes appear in **bold**. Here is an example: "When clicking the **Clear completed** button, all the tasks will be removed from the list because it's a to-do list application, so completed tasks shouldn't appear on it."

> **Tips or important notes**
> Appear like this.

Get in touch

Feedback from our readers is always welcome.

General feedback: If you have questions about any aspect of this book, email us at customercare@packtpub.com and mention the book title in the subject of your message.

Errata: Although we have taken every care to ensure the accuracy of our content, mistakes do happen. If you have found a mistake in this book, we would be grateful if you would report this to us. Please visit www.packtpub.com/support/errata and fill in the form.

Piracy: If you come across any illegal copies of our works in any form on the internet, we would be grateful if you would provide us with the location address or website name. Please contact us at copyright@packt.com with a link to the material.

If you are interested in becoming an author: If there is a topic that you have expertise in and you are interested in either writing or contributing to a book, please visit authors.packtpub.com.

Share Your Thoughts

Once you've read *Redux Made Easy with Rematch*, we'd love to hear your thoughts! Scan the QR code below to go straight to the Amazon review page for this book and share your feedback.

https://packt.link/r/1801076219

Your review is important to us and the tech community and will help us make sure we're delivering excellent quality content.

Section 1: Rematch Essentials

On completion of this part, you will be able to understand why and how Redux was created. You'll learn what the motivations were for creating Rematch and how it works internally. Also, you'll learn how to create a simple to-do app with Vanilla JavaScript with Redux, and to close the section, you'll migrate that application to Rematch.

In this section, we include the following chapters:

- *Chapter 1, Why Redux? An Introduction to Redux Architecture*
- *Chapter 2, Why Rematch over Redux? An Introduction to Rematch Architecture*
- *Chapter 3, Redux First Steps – Creating a Simple To-Do App*
- *Chapter 4, From Redux to Rematch – Migrating a To-Do App to Rematch*

1
Why Redux? An Introduction to Redux Architecture

Redux is a consolidated state management solution used by millions of websites, downloaded 3 million times per week. Overall, it's a great solution for a complex problem, but it was created with some limitations that Rematch aims to solve with best practices.

In this book, we'll analyze the weakest points of Redux and how Rematch solves them with a small wrapper in less than 2 KB. We'll move from the most basic example of a to-do task application to an Amazon clone website built with React and latest web technologies trends. We'll also create a mobile application with React Native and Rematch, introduce testing coverage, and, of course, explore TypeScript and Rematch plugins. By the end of this book, you'll be able to create any application or migrate an existing one to Rematch.

In this chapter, we'll learn why Redux was created and what problem it is designed to solve. Also, we'll learn how it works internally, and we'll get acquainted with some Redux terminology.

In this chapter, we will cover the following topics:

- Why Redux?
- What was there before Redux?
- How does Redux work?

By the end of this chapter, you will know the story behind Redux, how it works internally, and what was the cause of its creation. Of course, you will also learn practically all the most important terminology of Redux and use it in the next chapters.

Technical requirements

To follow along with this chapter, all you will need is a basic knowledge of ES6 JavaScript.

Why Redux?

To get started with this book, it's interesting to know what Redux does and what problem it's designed to solve.

In 2015, **Redux** was created by Dan Abramov, who began writing the first Redux implementation while preparing for a conference talk at React Europe, and Andrew Clark. Redux is a predictable state container for JavaScript applications; in other words, it is a utility tool to manage global states, which means data that is reachable across many parts of your application.

Where I used to work, we always asked the same question before starting a project: do we really need Redux? The problem we found is that when your application gets more complex, with more components that need to pass props down from a parent component to child components, the more complex the project becomes to read and improve. In short, it becomes unmaintainable.

This is an example of a common architecture of a basic application that passes down props from a parent component to child components:

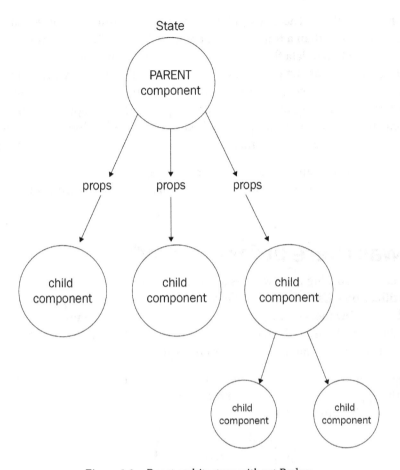

Figure 1.1 – React architecture without Redux

That's where Redux joins the game. Redux eases these complexities, providing patterns and tools that make it easier to understand when, where, why, and how the state will be updated, and how your application logic will behave when those changes occur.

Redux will help when we need to do the following tasks:

- Manage large amounts of application state that are needed in many places.
- Manage business logic that is complex to update.
- Create an app that will be maintained by many people.

A year after releasing React, Facebook published the **Flux architecture** on social media. Flux is more of a pattern than a framework; it eschews **Model-View-Controller** (**MVC**) in favor of a unidirectional data flow. When a user interacts with the user interface, the user interface propagates an action through a singleton dispatcher to many stores that hold the application's data, which updates all of the user interfaces that are affected. Flux architecture became really popular, and so many implementations appeared, too, but the most popular was Redux; the adoption of Redux was quickly adopted by the React community, and it soon became common to teach the use of React and Redux together.

Now that we know why Redux is interesting for our projects and why it was created, we should look at what frontend technologies for state management existed before Redux entered the game.

What was there before Redux?

In 2011, Facebook had a big issue with its notification system; the problem was called **Zombie Notifications**. Users received chat notifications, but when they clicked on them, there would be no new messages waiting for them. The Facebook team was getting a lot of complaints about this issue, and after a lot of research, they found the problem: the entire architecture was weak and had been since its creation.

Facebook was using the MVC architecture at the time, which became increasingly unstable as the application grew more and more complex. Here's an example of a common MVC architecture:

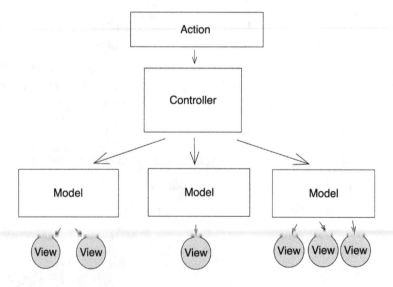

Figure 1.2 – MVC architecture

Basically, the number of models, controllers, and views that shaped Facebook became unmanageable to maintain. That's why newer frameworks appeared in the frontend ecosystem, one of which was **Backbone.js**.

Backbone.js was one of the first popular MVC frameworks that went viral around 2015. It acts as a smart wrapper around JavaScript objects and arrays and includes a small pub-sub events system built into it. Pub-sub is a publisher-subscriber relationship where the publisher sends a message to a topic and it is immediately received by the subscriber. All models and collections automatically trigger events as data is changed.

Here is an example of Backbone.js architecture:

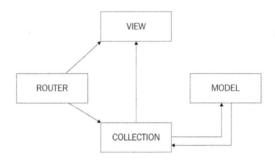

Figure 1.3 – Backbone.js architecture

We can compare Backbone.js with the MVC architecture in *Figure 1.2* and see how much easier Backbone.js was compared to an MVC architecture, but there was still work ahead to improve even more the state management solutions.

In 2014, Flux was adopted early by many people and this new method of state management was approved by developers. One of the main concepts of Flux is that *all data must flow in only one direction*. When the data flow is always in the same direction, everything is super predictable.

As we saw in *Figure 1.2*, some views and models have arrows running in both directions, so the data flow is bidirectional. With Flux, the MVC diagram is reconsidered, as shown in *Figure 1.4*:

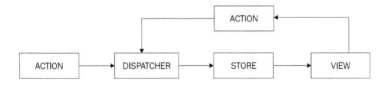

Figure 1.4 – Flux architecture

Let's briefly explain what the elements in each box mean.

Flux Actions

Actions are descriptions of the ways users can interact with the app. Basically, they are JavaScript objects, whose only requirement is to contain a required `type` field, although they do contain extra data used to fill the store.

Here is an example of a Flux action with the required `type` field and a `payload` object:

```
{
    "type": "ADD_TODO_ITEM",
    "payload": {
        "taskId": 1,
        "task": "Some task name"
    }
}
```

We use the `type` field to define what kind of change will be made to the app state, and `payload` is used for passing data to the store.

Flux Dispatcher

The **Dispatcher** function receives an action as an argument and forwards it to each of the application's stores. We have to remember that any Flux application with a solid pattern must only contain one dispatcher method.

To make it clear, we could say the dispatcher method is like a central interface between actions and stores. Basically, it is the magic wand that orchestrates actions and sends them directly to the store.

Here is an example of a Flux Dispatcher:

```
const countDispatcher = new CountDispatcher();
let countStore = {count:0}
countDispatcher.dispatch({ action: 'incrementCount' })
console.log(countStore)
// {count: 1}
```

This code is just an example of how a Flux `dispatch` function could be executed; the most common way is passing an object with the type that must match the reducer name. This is why we must think about dispatching actions such as triggering events – something happened, and we want the store to know about it.

Flux Stores

Stores contain the application state and logic. They are similar to a model in the MVC architecture.

A store registers itself with the dispatcher and provides it with a callback. This callback receives the action as a parameter, the store is subscribed to read any action that comes, and decides accordingly how to interpret that action. After the stores are updated, they broadcast an event declaring that their state has changed. In that way, the user interfaces can query the new state and repaint the screen correctly.

Basically, we have to understand that in order to modify our stores, we'll need to "dispatch" actions. Since all stores receive actions, a store will determine whether or not to modify its state upon receiving an action by looking at that action's type.

Views

Views (also called **user interfaces**) are what the user can see and interact with. They are the interfaces for displaying the data coming from our stores, as well as for sending actions back to the stores through the Dispatcher. Flux and Redux were designed to work with any frontend framework because there are **bindings**. A software binding refers to a mapping of one thing to another; it's like a wrapper to resolve the complexities of other libraries, but they were mainly designed to work with React.

For React there is a library called `react-redux`, a library for which you need to learn just one method for now: `connect()`. To be brief, because we'll explain this in detail in *Chapter 5*, *React with Rematch – The Best Couple – Part I*, `connect()` maps our Redux state to props on our React component. With this library, it becomes easier to integrate Redux into our React projects.

The following diagram depicts how React handles Redux subscriptions:

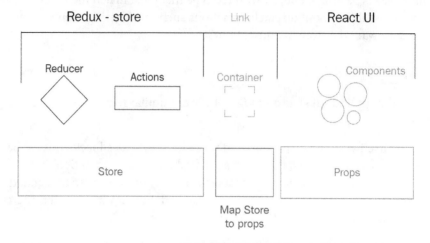

Figure 1.5 – React UI architecture with Redux

We can see the common architecture of Redux, but with the addition of a section called **Link** – this is where the react-redux `connect()` function makes the connection between React and Redux.

In this section, we learned how frontend technologies regarding state management evolved. We also learned how Flux works and why it was created, covering the main concepts to continue our journey with Redux. Now we are going to introduce and compare the main differences between Flux architecture and the refined way of Redux.

How does Redux work?

Flux is a generalized pattern of doing things, a reusable solution to a frequent problem in software architecture within a given situation. Redux is one of the frameworks that took this pattern and tweaked it to solve even more problems.

Redux and Flux both share the concern that you must concentrate your store update logic somewhere. In Flux, stores could be a good place to store the data and its logic, but in Redux, we use reducers because Redux only has a single store. This means that we only have one way to communicate with that source of truth, through actions that trigger reducers that update the store.

As we did with the Flux pattern, to help us compare the differences, let's see a diagram of the Redux architecture:

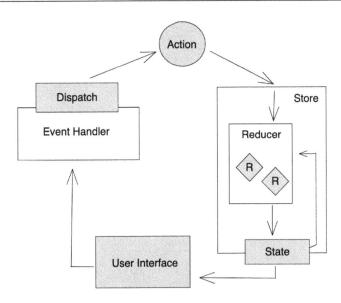

Figure 1.6 – Redux architecture

With Redux, the whole application state is placed within a centralized store that acts as the application's single source of truth. Also, the store becomes simpler because then it's only responsible for containing the state and is no longer in charge of determining how to adjust its state in response to actions – that logic is assigned to reducers.

Actions follow the same pattern in Flux as in Redux, which means we can now jump straight to reducers and stores.

Reducers

Reducers are just pure functions. Pure functions, by definition, are functions where the return value is always determined by its input values, which means that they are really predictable and testable. To clarify this, a pure function will never be a function with **side effects**. Side effects are usually AJAX requests, random numbers, mutations... because they introduce newer data that doesn't depend directly on its input values.

Reducers are simply functions that accept the current state as the first argument and the second argument as a given action. The output will be either the unmodified state or a new, edited copy of the state.

Another difference with Flux is that Redux assumes your state is immutable; that means you can't mutate your data. Reducers must always return the entire state (that means a new object reference), which is easy with the new object/array spread operator, a new proposal in JavaScript. This allows us to use the spread (...) operator to copy enumerable properties from one object to another in a simpler way.

Here's an example of a Redux reducer in code:

```
const todoAppReducer = (state = { tasks: [] }, action) => {
  switch (action.type) {
    case 'ADD_TODO_TASK':
      return {
        ...state,
        tasks: [
          ...state.tasks,
          action.payload
        ]
      }
    default: return state
  }
}
```

This reducer will read from an `action` argument with a payload, which is the new task that will be added to current state tasks. We use the spread operator to easily merge the current state with the new state.

Stores

Redux stores employ shallow equality checking, which simply entails checking that two different variables reference the same object. A shallow equality check that comes quickly to our minds is a simple a `===` b; therefore, they are immutable by default, which means you can't change the state directly. You must use reducers to make copies of existing objects/arrays, and modify the copies if needed, to finally return the new reference.

The main difference between Redux and Flux is that Redux only includes a single store per application instead of multiple stores, as Flux does. Having a single store makes persisting and updating the user interface simpler and, of course, simplifies the subscription logic.

This doesn't mean that every piece of state in your application must be placed in a Redux store. You should decide whether a piece of state belongs in Redux or your user interface components. For example, if we build a little component with some internal configuration that just belongs to that component, it isn't a good practice to introduce that state into Redux – just keep it simple using the local state.

We already mentioned that *data must flow in only one direction*, which perfectly describes the steps to update our application UI.

When our application is rendered for the first time, the following occurs:

1. A store is created using a root reducer function.

2. The store calls the root reducer once and saves the return value as its initial state.

3. When the user interface is first rendered, our user interface will access our data inside the store and also subscribe to any future store updates to know whether the state has changed.

What about when we update something in the application? The application code must dispatch an action to the Redux store like so:

```
store.dispatch({ type: "counter/increment" })
```

When the store receives the emitted action, the following occurs:

1. The store runs the reducer function again with the previous state and the current action and saves the return value as the new state.

2. The store notifies all parts of the user interface that subscribed previously.

3. Each component that has subscribed forces a re-render with the new data.

Unidirectional flow is the concept key that Redux offers against other state management solutions, it's predictable by default. Because you can't ever mutate the application state, all the changes in our state are done through reducers, which are invoked through actions, creating a predictable state, since the consequence of an action will result in a concrete state:

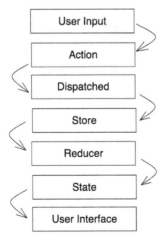

Figure 1.7 – Redux unidirectional data flow

Creating a state that is predictable means that by using Redux, we will know what every single action in our application will do and how the state will change when this action is received.

Summary

In this chapter, we have learned the main differences between Flux and Redux and understood the key concepts needed to start a simple application with Redux. Understanding these concepts and terminology will allow you to follow along with the next chapters related to Rematch without any problems.

In the next chapter, we will learn why Rematch was created on top of Redux, and what problems it tries to solve.

2
Why Rematch over Redux? An Introduction to Rematch Architecture

In this chapter, we'll briefly analyze the reasons why Rematch was created. We'll also see how Rematch works internally and how it's possible to reduce Redux boilerplate with Rematch. We'll learn how Rematch, despite being less than 2 kilobytes in size, can reduce the code that we need to set up Redux by 90%.

This chapter is important for understanding the key concepts of Rematch that we'll be looking at in the next few chapters.

In this chapter, we will cover the following topics:

- Why Rematch?
- How does Rematch work?

By the end of this chapter, you will be able to understand any Rematch concept as well as understand why Rematch was created and how the developer experience gets improved by using the latest JavaScript features.

Technical requirements

To follow along with this chapter, all you will need is a basic knowledge of ES6 JavaScript.

Why Rematch?

Rematch was created in 2017 by Shawn McKay and Blair Bodnar, a pair of Canadian programmers who thought that Redux should be simpler and easier to use.

As McKay said in several publications, Rematch is a wrapper around Redux that provides a simpler API, without losing any of the configurability that Redux offers.

We saw in the previous chapter that Redux has a steep learning curve compared to a simple component local state because it includes so much new terminology and so many features that don't exist in other development suites.

As regards Redux, we can use this formula to easily understand why an abstraction layer is necessary:

$$\frac{time\_saved}{time\_invested} = quality\_of\_api$$

Figure 2.1 – Formula to calculate the quality of our API for managing state

time_saved represents the time you may have spent developing your own state management solution, while **time_invested** is the hours invested in reading documentation, watching tutorials, and researching unfamiliar terminologies and different concepts.

quality_of_api is calculated by dividing **time_saved** by **time_invested**. We can easily see that with Redux, we will spend a lot of time learning unfamiliar terminologies, new libraries, and new standards for operating with Redux, so we will end up with a poor quality project code base. The time we could save by using Redux instead of creating our own state management solution actually gets lost because of the time that needs to be invested in learning new technologies. That's the main reason to consider Rematch as a wrapper around Redux.

We understand that the main purpose of any library is to make something complicated seem simple through abstraction, that is, hiding the underlying complexity through simpler functions – that's what Rematch does. With Rematch, we try to reduce **time_invested** to the smallest possible amount using a little abstraction layer.

Refactoring Redux is impossible because it's used by millions of developers; you can't justify introducing breaking changes that will affect all those users. That's another reason to build something around Redux instead of modifying the Redux code base internally.

Here are some topics that we found complex when configuring a simple hypothetical to-do app with Redux.

Setting up a store

In a real-world application using Redux, the application can become unmaintainable pretty fast because of the need to "Redux Thunk" asynchronous actions.

For practically 90% of the ideas we will come up with when building an application, we need to consume data from external services. They aren't static because we always need dynamism in our websites, for instance, calling an API to recover data or save modification of this data in a database. When this requirement is met, a plain Redux store has limited capabilities. It can only handle the dispatching of basic actions, and provides no built-in capabilities for doing asynchronous logic.

Redux stores are configurable, and it's normal to add several additional configuration options for common use cases. Typically, a Redux store is configured to add middleware for async logic and enable or disable the Redux DevTools for debugging. Unfortunately, the configuration process usually takes several steps.

For this reason, you'll need to set up the following:

- **Middleware:** Provides a third-party extension point between the dispatch of an action and the moment it reaches the reducer.

- **Composing:** A tool included in Redux to produce a single function from multiple functions.

  We can avoid chaining functions like this:

  ```
  func1(func2(func3(func4())))
  ```

  Instead, we can use the `compose()` method to produce the same result:

  ```
  compose(func1, func2, func3, func4)
  ```

  These two lines of code are equivalent; only the syntax differs.

All this does is let you write deeply nested function transformations without any rightward drift of the code. Its intention is to help you to do things easier, but it just means more terminology to know and more code to maintain.

In Rematch, these concepts are no longer required to start a real application and are resolved internally in a modern way. The Redux Toolkit package simplifies the typical setup process down to just a function, like Rematch does, which is why these examples are based on the old Redux that has been there for a long time.

We'll learn all the required concepts to start a new application with Rematch or migrate an old Redux code base to Rematch.

To explain, here is an example of a real Redux store:

```
import { createStore, applyMiddleware, compose } from Redux
import thunk from "redux-thunk"
import api from "../middlewares/api"
import rootReducer from "../reducers"
import devTools from "../containers/DevTools"

const store = (preloadedState) => createStore(
  rootReducer,
  preloadedState,
  compose(
    applyMiddleware(
      thunk,
      api
    ),
    devTools.instrument()
  ),
)
```

This code is a demonstration of how Redux becomes complex and introduces so much code just for storing data, even for simple applications. We need to use three different imports (compose, applyMiddleware, and thunk) for handling asynchronous operations, and this is just for initializing the store.

In Rematch, we simplify the previous setup to this:

```
import { init } from "@rematch/core"
import models from "./models"

const store = init({
  redux: { initialState: { } },
  models,
})
```

As you can see, Rematch handles all the complex things required to start developing your application.

Reducers

Reducers in Redux usually, and not always, contain a switch for routing the `action` type, which becomes larger and larger when our application starts to grow.

Redux itself doesn't care what control flow logic you use inside a reducer. You could use an `if/else` statement, lookup tables, or whatever you want. In Rematch, we try to simplify this decision to just keep the reducers as simple as possible, just an object with reducers that accepts `state` as the first parameter and `payload` as the second. The state is automatically filled by Rematch, so you don't have to worry about passing it to each reducer.

Here is an example of a Redux reducer:

```
const todoAppReducer = (state = { tasks: [] } action) => {
  switch (action.type) {
    case 'ADD_TODO_TASK':
      return {
        ...state,
        tasks: [
          ...state.tasks,
          action.payload
        ]
      }
    default: return state
  }
}
```

And here is an example of a Rematch reducer:

```
const todoAppReducer = {
  ADD_TODO_TASK: (state, action) => ({ ...state, tasks:
  [...state.tasks, action.payload] })
}
```

We can compare the two code blocks and see that we have improved our code base in three ways:

- We decreased the lines of code from 13 to 3 lines, a 125% variation. From this, you can imagine the massive improvements that Rematch can make to a really complex Redux application.

- By reducing the amount of code, we increased its legibility, and when using the latest ES6 features, you will find that Rematch is easier to read and understand.

- Moving from `action.type` and a `switch` statement to just having keys inside an object makes everything easier (from refactoring the code to testing it).

In Rematch, reducers are just pure functions with two arguments – the state and an optional payload – and must always return a new state reference.

With this concept clear, we can jump into asynchronous operations. We'll learn how Rematch handles async operations without the need to use external libraries, as well as looking at the best ES6 techniques.

Async/await over Redux Thunk

Thunks are used to create asynchronous actions in Redux. In many ways, a Thunk seems more like a workaround hack than an official solution:

1. You dispatch an action, which is actually a function rather than the expected object.
2. The Thunk middleware checks every action to see whether it is a function.
3. If so, the middleware calls the function and passes access to some store methods, such as `dispatch` and `getState()`.

With ES2017, `async/await` was introduced, which is a special syntax to work with Promises in a more modern and easier way compared to ES5.

Rematch makes things a bit easier for writing these types of operations, Redux needs an outer function, called a thunk action creator. Rematch, instead, does this automatically for you when effects are created, so you can write just `async`/`await` inside the `effects` property and not worry about anything else.

This code is an example of an asynchronous request inside an outer function called `saveNewTodo`, in this way we're able to do the side-effect operation:

```
export function saveNewTodo(text) {
    return async function saveNewTodoThunk(dispatch, getState) {
        const initialTodo = { text }
        const response = await client.post('/fakeApi/todos', {
        todo: initialTodo })
        dispatch({ type: 'todos/todoAdded', payload: response.todo
})
    }
}
```

The problem with this code is the complexity of understanding why we need to wrap an `async` function with another function just to pass a text payload. Doing so is mandatory because Redux Thunk doesn't accept more arguments other than the `async` functions, so you need to wrap the `async` function with another function to finally pass the text argument.

Rematch solves this by extracting the `dispatch` parameter to an outside function:

```
const todos = {
    effects: (dispatch) => ({
        async saveNewTodo(text) {
            const response = await client.post('/fakeApi/todos', {
            todo: text })
            dispatch.todos.todoAdded(response.todo)
        }
    })
}
```

This Rematch code is equivalent to the Redux Thunk code, but this code is self-descriptive. You can see that we use the `dispatch` function that is filled automatically by Rematch as the first argument of the effects property and then we created an `async` function that accepts a text argument as a payload. Now you can begin to understand why Redux needed a wrapper and why Rematch performs complex operations much more smoothly.

Reducers and effects

When we think about actions that must happen in our application, there are two kinds of actions to consider:

- **Reducers**: Trigger a reducer and return a new state.
- **Effects**: Trigger async actions that could call a reducer to change the state.

Thinking about things in this way can be less confusing than using Redux Thunk. In Rematch, our models only contain states, reducers, and effects. If we need something more complex, we can use Rematch plugins.

Folder structure

Since Redux is just a state management solution, it has no direct opinion on how our projects should be structured. However, over time, we saw that many of the tutorials we could find on the internet chose the strategy of creating folders by type, and much of the actual code written with Redux is written like this.

With such a folder structure, we would end up changing code in the **actions** folder and forgetting to change the code in the **reducers** folder as well; that's why Rematch tries to encapsulate actions and reducers in the same file.

Nowadays, this is no longer the recommended technique and the Redux team has worked on teaching the **ducks pattern**. This pattern stipulates that reducers, action types, and actions should co-exist in a single file, something similar to what Rematch encourages.

Here's an example of a folder structure for a Redux to-do app:

Figure 2.2 – Redux folder structure

Here it is with Rematch:

Figure 2.3 – Rematch folder structure

In summary, we have learned that writing Redux logic by hand requires extra work that isn't necessary, and an abstraction layer can help simplify that process. Rematch was designed to offer a simple and viable alternative to something complex that should have been simple.

In the next section, we'll analyze how Rematch works internally and the main concepts that you need to know about getting started with using it.

How does Rematch work?

Internally, Rematch is pretty simple. That's why calling it a framework isn't quite correct; it's just a higher layer without the Redux boilerplate.

Let's analyze Rematch in depth. In *Figure 2.4*, we introduce the Rematch model:

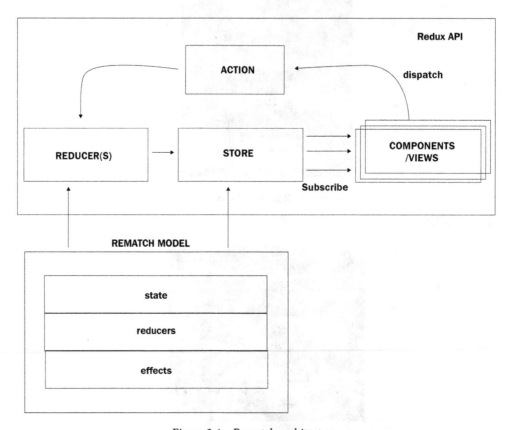

Figure 2.4 – Rematch architecture

Rematch models are among the most important parts of your store because they allow you to define the initial state of the model, the reducers, and the effects.

Any model is built on the basis of these properties:

Name

Models can contain a name that will become a key in the Redux store – this means that you will be able to access the state of a model or dispatch actions from a model using its name. Now, a name is not mandatory – if you don't provide a name, Rematch will use the object keys provided to the `init()` function instead.

The `init()` function returns a Rematch store, which is essentially a Redux store with a few additional properties and some extra features for doing certain things more easily.

Here is a mock example of the `init()` function:

```
import { init } from '@rematch/core'

const store = init({
  name: 'my custom store name',
  models: { example1, example2 },
  plugins: [plugin1, plugin2],
  redux: customReduxConfig,
})
```

`init()` functions accept four properties:

- `name`: We can name the store using this; this can be super useful when creating multiple stores for testing purposes.
- `models`: This is the property where we define the models that are going to be running inside our store. It's an object that contains models. If the model contains a `name` property, that will be the key; if not, the model name will be the object key.
- `plugins`: This is an array of functions that can extend the functionality of your store. We have several plugins developed by the Rematch team, plus an API for creating a new one (we'll analyze this in *Chapter 9, Composable Plugins – Create Your First Plugin*).
- `redux`: This is an object with which you can access the Redux API configuration. It is useful when migrating from complex Redux setups to Rematch as you can preserve your configurations inside this property.

With this clear, we return back to the model's schema:

```
export const todoModel = {
  name: "todoModel",
}
```

We can overwrite the model's name using the `name` property inside our model object. Now, let's look at what every model must contain.

State

Every model must contain a `state` property, used primarily for defining the initial state of a model. In the following snippet, we introduce a state:

```
export const todoModel = {
  name: "todoModelName",
  state: {
    tasks: [],
  }
}
```

We are initializing this model with an empty array of tasks that could be filled, accessed, or cleared from our reducers.

Reducers

The `reducers` property is an object of n functions that change the model's state. These functions always have two parameters – the previous state and the payload – and must always return the model's next state.

These functions should be pure functions, as explained in the previous chapter. If we need to use async methods or some complex logic, we can use effects instead. The effects property of our model allows us to introduce side effects without any performance limitations or any bad practice.

Following on from the previous snippet, we can introduce some reducers:

```
export const todoModel = {
  name: "todoModelName",
  state: {
    tasks: [],
  },
  reducers: {
    ADD_TODO_TASK: (state, payload) => ({
      ...state,
      tasks: [
        ...state.tasks,
        payload
      ]
```

```
    }),
    REMOVE_TASK: (state, payload) => ({
      ...state,
      tasks: state.tasks.filter((task) => task.id !== payload)
    })
  }
}
```

In this code snippet, we introduced two reducers:

- `ADD_TODO_TASK`: This is a pure function that returns the previous state with a new `tasks` array, with the new task that we passed in the `payload` parameter.
- `REMOVE_TASK`: This is a pure function returning the previous state, but that removes the desired task from the tasks state. For example, we could pass the ID of the task to remove as `payload`.

We can see that replacing the `switch` statements with simple functions inside an object called `reducers` simplifies reading and development. In the next section, we are going to see how effects work in a hypothetical example of recovering tasks from an external API.

Effects

The `effects` property is automatically filled with a `dispatch` parameter that could be used on any function that's inside our `effects` property to pass data to our reducers or to call other `effects` functions from other models.

Every function that appears in the scope of the `effects` property will be filled with two parameters:

- `payload`: Useful for passing extra arguments to this function; we will use it when we need to pass an ID for filtering or pass some data that isn't in our store.
- `rootState`: Contains the application state.

Effects have access to the whole state and all reducers; they allow us to handle impure functions with just async/await.

What if we need to recover some tasks from an external API? We must use effects because reducer functions should be kept as pure as possible.

Following the previous snippet, we will now introduce an effect for recovering a task from an external API:

```
export const todoModel = {
  name: "todoModelName",
  state: {
    tasks: [],
  },
  reducers: {
    ADD_TODO_TASK: (state, payload) => ({
      ...state,
      tasks: [
        ...state.tasks,
        payload
      ]
    }),
    REMOVE_TASK: (state, payload) => ({
      ...state,
      tasks: state.tasks.filter((task) => task.id !== payload)
    })
  },
  effects: (dispatch) => ({
    async getONETask() {
      const response = await fetch("http://local:3000/task/1")
      const oneTask = await response.json()
      dispatch.todoModelName.ADD_TODO_TASK(oneTask)
    }
  })
}
```

As you can see, we introduced an `effects` function property in our model that passes a `dispatch` parameter, filled with all the reducers and effects of our store. You can easily call other reducers, or other effects in other models, through this model name. Basically, Rematch creates a global structure where you can call any function of any model.

Imagine a scenario where there are three models with this structure:

```
const MODEL_ONE = {
    state: 0,
    reducers: {
        increment: (state) => state + 1
    }
}

const MODEL_TWO = {
    state: 0,
    reducers: {
        decrement: (state) => state - 1
    }
}
```

In this code, we're creating two Rematch models without effects, just with a state and a reducer function: one model for increasing the state value of MODEL_ONE, and the other for decreasing the state value of MODEL_TWO.

When Rematch is initialized, it automatically fills the dispatch parameter with access to any reducer or effect that is defined in our store models.

We could now create a third model with an effect calling the increment() reducer from MODEL_ONE and the decrement() reducer from MODEL_TWO:

```
const MODEL_THREE = {
    state: 0,
    effects: (dispatch) => ({
        firstFn() {
            dispatch.MODEL_ONE.increment()
            dispatch.MODEL_TWO.decrement()
        }
    })
}
```

In this code, we're accessing the dispatch parameter and increasing the state value of MODEL_ONE, and decreasing the state value of MODEL_TWO directly from another model, in this case, MODEL_THREE.

When this effect is dispatched through the global dispatch of our store, we have the following:

```
Store.dispatch({ type: "MODEL_THREE/firstFn" })
```

In this code snippet, we're using a hypothetical scenario where our MODEL_THREE effect is initialized in our Redux store, so we can dispatch our MODEL_THREE effect called firstFn().

We can check that our state has changed to this:

```
{
    "MODEL_ONE": 1
    "MODEL_TWO": -1
    "MODEL_THREE": 0
}
```

As we can see, the states of MODEL_ONE and MODEL_TWO changed correctly.

With all these concepts now clear, we can build anything from a small application to a big enterprise application.

Summary

In this chapter, we have learned about the main concepts that are required to start a simple application with Rematch. We also learned why Redux needs an abstraction layer and how Rematch entered the game to solve that problem.

Now that we've covered all these concepts, we can safely face the creation of our first application. We will learn how to create a simple Redux to-do application with vanilla JavaScript, for a future migration to Rematch.

3

Redux First Steps – Creating a Simple To-Do App

In this chapter, we'll learn how to create a real Redux to-do app, where we can introduce unlimited tasks to a list, remove them individually, toggle between completed and pending tasks, and, of course, remove all the completed ones.

This chapter is really important for understanding how plain vanilla Redux works. We use plain vanilla Redux to demonstrate more clearly how Rematch abstracts some of these concepts, and we'll also focus on learning about some important terminology and concepts of Rematch, such as initializing stores, writing reducers, or dispatching actions.

In this chapter, we will cover the following topics:

- Preparing the environment
- Creating our first store
- Creating our first reducer
- Dispatching actions

By the end of this chapter, you'll be able to create a real Redux to-do tasks application with real functionalities just by applying the theory we covered in previous chapters.

Technical requirements

To follow along with this chapter, you will need the following:

- Basic knowledge of Vanilla JavaScript and ES6 features
- Basic knowledge of HTML5 features
- A browser (Chrome or Firefox, for instance)
- A code editor (Visual Studio Code, for instance)

You can find the code for this chapter in the book's GitHub repository at `https://github.com/PacktPublishing/Redux-Made-Easy-with-Rematch/tree/main/packages/chapter-3`.

Preparing the environment

Redux can be used in practically any user interface layer that exists. To start this chapter, we'll build a simple to-do app with Vanilla JavaScript; that means that we'll use plain JavaScript without any additional libraries such as React or jQuery.

In this chapter, we won't need any bundlers such as Webpack. Webpack is a module bundler, which means its main purpose is bundling all of your JavaScript files, style files, and assets to make static assets that can be served directly, for instance, static HTML files. We will need Webpack in the following chapters to make React work with Redux and some external libraries. Using Webpack to bundle websites is commonplace in real-world apps, but for this introduction to Redux, we can explain things without it.

Redux ships **Universal Module Definition** (**UMD**) builds. This means that all the code provided by Redux in the distributable package will work on both frontend and backend environments. On the frontend side, UMD builds can be used directly within a `<script/>` source tag without Webpack.

To prepare the environment, we'll just need a text editor for writing our HTML code and JavaScript files, and a browser for seeing the changes. The editor I've recommended a lot is Visual Studio Code (`https://code.visualstudio.com`); it comes with IntelliSense, which is an amazing feature that provides smart completion based on variable types, function definitions, imported modules, and an ecosystem of extensions/plugins.

Once downloaded and installed, I recommend improving your development experience by installing this super useful extension, **Live Server**:

Figure 3.1 – Live Server for Visual Studio Code

This extension launches a local development server that allows you to see any changes without requiring you to reload the browser page.

To install it, we just need to click on the **Extensions** section of Visual Code Studio, search for **Live Server**, and press the green **Install** button.

Now, we're ready to start creating our first `index.html` file. HTML is a markup language that your browser uses to determine how a website should be displayed, while `index` indicates that it is the default web page of this directory of our website.

Inside the `index.html` file, we must write this code:

```
<!DOCTYPE html>
<html lang="en">
<head>
  <meta charset="UTF-8">
  <meta name="viewport" content="width=device-width, initial-
  scale=1.0">
  <title>Document</title>
</head>
<body>
  <h1>Redux Example</h1>
</body>
</html>
```

This code is the minimum amount of code required to make an `index.html` file work on the browser. The `<head>` element is the container of all the information about the document. In this case, we're adding a charset for compatibility with the UTF-8 charset, a viewport for compatibility with mobile browsers, and a title for our website. The `<body>` tag is used to add all the HTML elements; there can only be one `<body>` tag per `<html>` element.

To check that our HTML is valid, we can run the Live Server extension:

Figure 3.2 – The Go Live button on the Visual Studio Code toolbar

Pressing the **Go Live** button will automatically open our default browser with the code we had written previously:

Redux Example

Figure 3.3 – Demo of the expected behavior, showing "Redux Example"

If we make any changes to the `index.html` file, the browser must refresh instantly and update the page with the corresponding changes.

Now we're ready to introduce Redux dependencies and initialize the first store. Also, we'll see how to check that everything is set up properly by accessing the Inspector tools of our browser.

Creating our first store

To be able to use Redux features inside our `index.html` file, we need to import the Redux library. There are several ways of doing this, from downloading the code locally and importing it via a `<script />` source tag, to installing it with a package manager such as **npm**.

Between the options of using npm or downloading the code locally, there is a tool called **unpkg**, a global content delivery network for everything that is published on npm. With this, we can easily load any file from any package using a URL.

So, let's modify the previous HTML snippet:

```
<!DOCTYPE html>
<html lang="en">
<head>
  <meta charset="UTF-8">
  <meta name="viewport" content="width=device-width, initial-
  scale=1.0">
```

```
    <title>Document</title>
  </head>
  <body>
    <h1>Redux Example</h1>
    <script src="https://unpkg.com/redux@latest"></script>
  </body>
</html>
```

As you can see, we included an `unpkg` URL to include the latest Redux library inside our `index.html` file before closing the `body` tag.

To check that we wrote the import correctly and that everything is working as expected, we can open **Inspect Tools/Console** and write the following:

```
window.Redux
```

Then, we should see something like this:

Redux Example

Figure 3.4 – Redux has been injected correctly

Our application will be a to-do app, so we have to make sure that our user interface contains the following:

- A basic form: `<form>`, `<label>`
- Some input text: `<input>`
- A button to submit: `<button>`
- A list to display the to-do tasks: `<ul>`, `<li>`
- A button to clear completed tasks: `<button>`

With our requirements covered by HTML elements, we can start creating the user interface:

```html
<!DOCTYPE html>
<html lang="en">
<head>
  <meta charset="UTF-8">
  <meta name="viewport" content="width=device-width, initial-scale=1.0">
  <title>Document</title>
</head>
<body>
  <h1>Redux Example</h1>
  <ul id="todos-container"></ul>
  <form id="add-todo">
    <label for="add">To-do title</label> <input id="add" name="todoText" />
    <button>Submit</button>
  </form>
  <button id="clear-todos">Clear completed</button>
  <script src="https://unpkg.com/redux@latest"></script>
</body>
</html>
```

Now, we should see something like this:

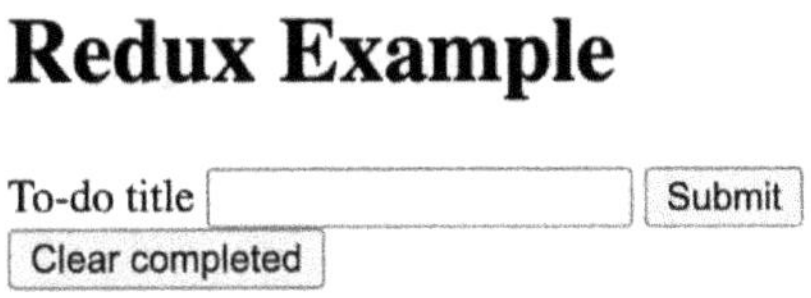

Redux Example

To-do title [   ] [Submit]
[Clear completed]

Figure 3.5 – HTML rendered on the browser

The `<ul>` element isn't displayed because there are no to-do tasks yet; we'll create them dynamically thanks to Redux subscription methods. Now, let's move on to write our first JavaScript file and initialize the store.

Create a `todo-app.js` file in the root folder and import it underneath our Redux `<script>` import:

```
<!DOCTYPE html>
<html lang="en">
<head>
  <meta charset="UTF-8">
  <meta name="viewport" content="width=device-width, initial-
  scale=1.0">
  <title>Document</title>
</head>
<body>
  <h1>Redux Example</h1>
  <script src="https://unpkg.com/redux@latest"></script>
  <script src="./todo-app.js"></script>
</body>
</html>
```

Now, all the code we introduce inside the `todo-app.js` file will be executed on the first render of the website. We could create unlimited JavaScript files and add them in the same way.

Initializing the store is pretty simple with Redux. You just need to call the `createStore()` method of Redux, passing a pure function as the first parameter:

```
function reducer(state, action) {
  return {
    todos: []
  }
```

```
}
```

```
const store = window.Redux.createStore(reducer);
store.subscribe(render);
```

```
function render() {}
```

As we have already introduced the `store.subscribe()` method, this method will re-run the function passed each time that a value inside our store changes.

We can check that everything is working correctly by installing an amazing extension for our browser: **Redux DevTools**. Redux DevTools is a tool for debugging an application's state changes in a more visual way, which will help us on our journey through Redux development. Also, Rematch works out of the box with this extension.

Once Redux DevTools has been installed, we have to add an extra line to our `createStore` function to make sure it works:

```
const store = window.Redux.createStore(
  reducer,
  window.__REDUX_DEVTOOLS_EXTENSION__ && window.__REDUX_
  DEVTOOLS_EXTENSION__()
);
```

Now, we can easily check the **State** tab to see that our store has been initialized correctly with an empty `todos` array:

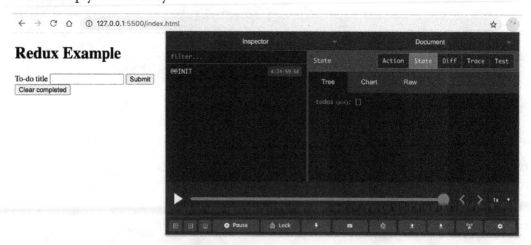

Figure 3.6 – Redux DevTools demonstration of an empty todos array

Creating a store is really useful because it will be where all the data will be located, but we need some extra code to introduce or remove data from this store. This is where reducers enter the game.

Creating our first reducer

As we saw in *Chapter 1, Why Redux? An Introduction to Redux Architecture*, in the *How does Redux work?* section, our logic must be introduced inside a reducer function. Let's identify exactly what the main objective of our application is so we can come up with actions that suit those objectives – we need our application to do the following:

- Add a task.

- Remove a to-do task.

- Toggle tasks to show as completed.

- Clear completed tasks.

We will look at each of these points in detail now.

Adding a task

Adding a task to our store means pushing a new task to our `todos` array. This is important so that we know what code we must introduce inside our reducer.

Firstly, we can agree on the schema that will contain our tasks. This definition will be used throughout the application, so remember that our tasks will always include an ID, a title, and a `completed` check:

```
{
    "id": id,
    "title": string,
    "completed": boolean
}
```

Now, let's modify the reducer to react when an action with the `ADD_TODO` type is received:

```
const INITAL_STATE = {
  todos: []
}
function reducer(state = INITAL_STATE, action) {
  switch(action.type) {
```

```
    case "ADD_TODO": {
      const newTodo = {
        id: action.id,
        title: action.title,
        completed: false,
      }
      return {
        ...state,
        todos: [...state.todos, newTodo]
      }
    }
    default: return state
  }
}
```

Let's understand the code step by step. First, we defined a constant called INITIAL_STATE for handling the initial state of our reducer.

You can see that there's a switch statement to return the initial state in case no conditions are met, basically, an action.type property not defined in the switch statement. This is really useful for the first render of our application when no actions are dispatched so that we can define an initial state for our application.

We modified our reducer function to include a switch with a single case, adding a task. As we saw previously in our schema, a task appears with id, a title value coming from the HTML form, and the completed field set to false by default. To conclude the logic of our reducer, we must always return a new reference of the state, so we returned the new state with a new todos array with the new task that we created in the newTodo constant.

We can't do a state.todos.push(newTodo) method directly because .push() doesn't change the reference of the state and Redux can't know whether the state has changed. There are some libraries, such as Immer and Immutable.js, that fix this condition, which we'll see in *Chapter 8, The Rematch Plugins Ecosystem*.

Removing a to-do task

Removing a task from a list can be complex, but it's pretty easy if we use JavaScript methods such as `filter()`. To add a new case, we just need to introduce a new action type to our `switch` statement:

```
case "REMOVE_TASK": {
  const newTodos = state.todos.filter(todo =>
    todo.id !== action.id
  );
  return {...state, todos: newTodos }
}
```

This code is practically self-explanatory – we're getting all the to-do tasks that are in the state and filtering them by the `action.id` value that is passed. This will return all the states that are not equal to the `id` value that's passed, which is the same as removing a to-do task.

Toggling tasks to show as completed

What if we want to change the value of a current to-do task that already exists in the store?

As we did in the previous sections, we can add a new action type to our `switch` statement:

```
case "TOGGLE_COMPLETED": {
  const newTodos = state.todos.map(todo =>
    todo.id === action.id ? { ...todo, completed: !todo.
    completed } : todo
  );
  return { ...state, todos: newTodos };
}
```

Instead of using `.filter()` as in the previous case, we're using a `.map()` method. The `.map()` method creates a new array, which is the important part, because it makes Redux forget the previous reference, populating the results of a specific function on every element in the calling array. If we use `.forEach()` instead, or a simple `for` loop, this won't work because we'll preserve the same reference.

Inside the `.map()` function, we're using a ternary expression; this is an `if-else` statement, but is only one line long. If `action.id` is equal to `todo.id` (meaning we found the element that we want to modify), we return the task with the opposite value of the `completed` property; if not, the task is just returned.

Clearing completed tasks

`CLEAR_COMPLETED` is similar to `REMOVE_TASK`, but we won't need an action payload; we just need to filter the tasks that have been completed already:

```
case "CLEAR_COMPLETED": {
const filteredTodos = state.todos.filter(todo => !todo.
completed)
  return { ...state, todos: filteredTodos }
}
```

To summarize the previous four points, we have ended up with this reducer, which handles all the logic of our current to-do app:

```
const INITAL_STATE = {
  todos: []
}
function reducer(state = INITAL_STATE, action) {
  switch(action.type) {
    case "ADD_TODO": {
      const newTodo = {
        id: action.id,
        title: action.title,
        completed: false,
      }
      return {
        ...state,
        todos: [...state.todos, newTodo]
      }
    }
    case "REMOVE_TASK": {
      const newTodos = state.todos.filter(todo =>
        todo.id !== action.id
      );
```

```
        return {...state, todos: newTodos }
    }
    case "TOGGLE_COMPLETED": {
      const newTodos = state.todos.map(todo =>
        todo.id === action.id ? { ...todo, completed: !todo.
        completed } : todo
      );
      return { ...state, todos: newTodos };
    }
    case "CLEAR_COMPLETED": {
      const filteredTodos = state.todos.filter(todo => !todo.
      completed)
        return { ...state, todos: filteredTodos }
    }
    default: return state
  }
}
```

Now that we have the logic, we need to dispatch actions to that `switch` statement. But how are they dispatched? Well, via the `dispatch()` function inside our store.

Dispatching actions

Dispatching actions works in the same way for any action. Just running the `store.dispatch()` method will send the action to the reducer. You just need to pass an object as the first argument with the corresponding `type` property and the value.

We can start by triggering the action to add a new task to the state. Inside the `todo-app.js` file under `store.subscribe()`, we can add these lines of code that will handle how the form works:

```
const form = document.getElementById("add-todo");
form.addEventListener("submit", event => {
  event.preventDefault();
  const inputValue = event.target.elements.todoText.value;
  store.dispatch({
    type: "ADD_TODO",
    title: inputValue,
    id: Date.now()
```

```
    });
    event.target.elements.todoText.value = "";
});
```

Here, we're accessing the `form` element and adding an `eventListener` instance to listen when the submitted action occurs (this occurs natively when you include a button inside a form). We used `preventDefault()` to overwrite the default action that belongs to the event submitted. If we don't add `preventDefault()`, the page will be reloaded because that's the default browser action.

Next, we get the value of the input text accessing through the event target elements, and finally, we dispatch this value to our Redux `store` constant:

```
store.dispatch({
    type: "ADD_TODO",
    title: inputValue
    id: Date.now()
});
```

`type` must be the same as what appears in our `switch` statement inside our reducer function, while `title` is the value that will be inserted in the store, including the `id` and `completed` properties.

We can then check that everything worked, thanks to the Redux DevTools extension:

Figure 3.7 – Redux DevTools with an ADD_TODO action

Alright, we can see that the changes have been introduced correctly in the store, but how can we render the to-do tasks in the `<ul id="todos-container"></ul>` element?

When we initialized the store, we added the `store.subscribe(render)` method, so everything that's inside the `render()` function will be repainted when the state changes.

So, let's introduce some methods to create a list:

```
const todosContainer = document.getElementById("todos-
container");


function render() {
  todosContainer.innerHTML = "";
  const { todos } = store.getState();
  todos.forEach(todo => {
    const task = document.createElement("li");
    task.textContent = todo.title;
    todosContainer.appendChild(task);
  });
}
```

We should use `.getElementById()` outside of the `render()` function because the parent element, in our case, `todos-container`, won't change because it's just a wrapper for our content.

Introducing functions that access the **Document Object Model (DOM)** inside the `render()` function isn't optimal. When a website is loaded, the browser creates a DOM of the page. The DOM is like a tree of all the elements that we have added to our website and allows us to modify every element of our website via JavaScript functions, such as `.getElementById()`.

If we already know that our parent element, in our case, `todos-container`, won't change because it's a static element, we can extract the `.getElementById()` function outside of the `render()` function and the function `.getElementById()` will only run once because Redux, when it needs to repaint our screen, will execute the `render()` method. If we move this logic outside, this method will only run once. In the case of adding it inside, the `render()` function will be executed on every state change since Redux re-executes this method every time it needs to repaint something in the DOM. That wouldn't make any sense because we know that our parent element won't change, so it's totally unnecessary to get that element on every state change.

Getting an element from the DOM inside the render() function will be executed every time the data in our store changes, so if we already know that our parent element won't change, we can avoid re-computation and save ourselves a few milliseconds of rendering.

The main function is store.getState(). It returns all the state that is in the store and allows us to iterate the list and create one <li> element for each task.

If everything worked correctly, you should see something like this:

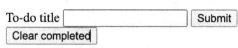

Redux Example

- works
- as
- expected

To-do title [   ] [Submit]
[Clear completed]

Figure 3.8 – How our example currently looks

Now, let's modify our render() function to introduce a new button to toggle the completed tasks and remove them from the list:

```
function render() {
  todosContainer.innerHTML = "";
  const { todos } = store.getState();
  todos.forEach(todo => {
    const task = document.createElement("li");
    task.textContent = todo.title;

    if (todo.completed) {
      task.style.textDecoration = "line-through";
    }
    createButton(task, "Remove", "REMOVE_TASK", todo.id);
    createButton(task, "Toggle done", "TOGGLE_COMPLETED", todo.id);

    todosContainer.appendChild(task);
  });
}
```

```
function createButton(parent, text, type, id) {
  const btn = document.createElement("button");
  btn.textContent = text;
  btn.addEventListener("click", () =>
    store.dispatch({ type, id })
  );
  parent.appendChild(btn);
}
```

We added an `if` statement to strike through the tasks that are already completed. Also, we created a simple function called `createButton` to create buttons and avoid the duplication of logic. This function is responsible for creating a button element, adding text content to the button, and dispatching the action.

With this code, we can now check whether our user interface is working properly:

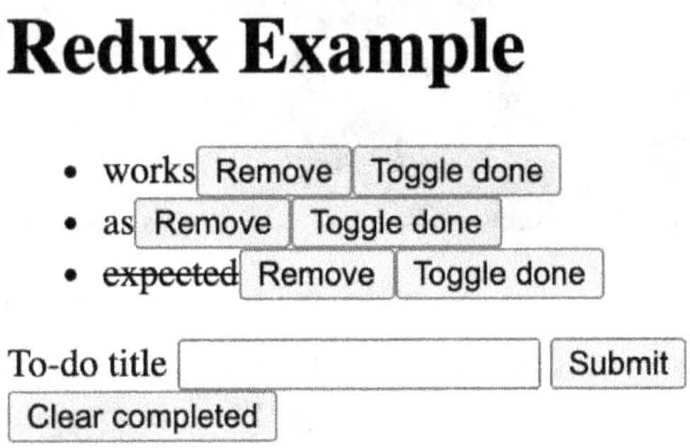

Redux Example

- works Remove | Toggle done
- as Remove | Toggle done
- ~~expected~~ Remove | Toggle done

To-do title [   ] Submit
Clear completed

Figure 3.9 – When clicking Toggle done, we can see that "expected" is struck through

There's just one requirement left: `CLEAR_COMPLETED`. In just two lines of code, we can add the logic to this feature:

```
const clearTodosButton = document.getElementById("clear-
todos");
clearTodosButton.addEventListener("click", () =>
  store.dispatch({ type: "CLEAR_COMPLETED" })
);
```

When clicking the **Clear completed** button, all the tasks will be removed from the list because it's a to-do list application, so completed tasks shouldn't appear on it.

Thanks to the Redux DevTools extension, we can jump between states and see how they change. This can be seen through the `action` methods, shown on the left of our Redux DevTools **Inspector** window:

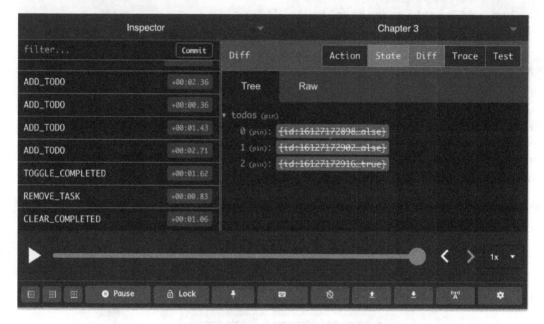

Figure 3.10 – Redux DevTools with full navigation functionality

As we worked through this section, we saw that using a single dispatcher reduces complexity and makes the state predictable through the action types.

Summary

In this chapter, we have learned how to create a real application for to-do tasks with real functionalities. We have also learned how Redux DevTools works and, most importantly, how the Redux architecture can be made to be predictable with a few steps.

In the next chapter, we will learn how to develop the same application but with Rematch best practices, as well as see how Rematch can turn something complex into an easy task, thereby reducing the learning curve.

4

From Redux to Rematch – Migrating a To-Do App to Rematch

In this chapter, we'll learn how to migrate the application that we have created to Rematch step by step. We'll see the main differences that we have already seen theoretically put into practice, and we'll see how Rematch simplifies our code base.

This chapter will explain the main changes that will be required for any type of application, from small ones to enterprise-grade ones, for a successful migration to Rematch.

Rematch simplifies migration in a few steps because, under the hood, it uses Redux internals, so practically all Redux code is compatible with Rematch. Some methods are renamed or simplified to be easier to use.

In this chapter, we will cover the following topics:

- Introducing the Rematch library
- Migrating a Redux store to Rematch init
- Migrating Redux reducers to Rematch reducers
- Migrating dispatch actions to effects

By the end of this chapter, we'll become proficient in refactoring Redux applications to Rematch, and we'll know intuitively which methods need to change and how to resolve all the conflicts.

Technical requirements

You will need the following to complete this chapter:

- Basic knowledge of ES6 features
- Basic knowledge of HTML5 features
- A browser (Chrome or Firefox, for instance)
- A code editor (Visual Studio Code, for instance)

You can find the code for this chapter in the book's GitHub repository at https://github.com/PacktPublishing/Redux-Made-Easy-with-Rematch/tree/main/packages/chapter-4.

Let's start by introducing the Rematch library and learning how to install it in our to-do website.

Introducing the Rematch library

To introduce the Rematch library in our application, we'll be using the same method that we used previously in *Chapter 3*, *Redux First Steps – Creating a Simple To-Do App*, in the *Creating our first store* section. As we did then, we will be using unpkg.com. Let's modify the `<script />` element under the closing body tag:

```
<script src="https://unpkg.com/redux@latest"></script>
<script src="https://unpkg.com/@rematch/core@latest"></script>
<script src="./todo-app.js"></script>
</body>
</html>
```

Rematch, like Redux, ships in a bundle with **ES Modules (ESM)**, **Common JS (CJS)**, and **Universal Module Definition (UMD)** builds. You can use Rematch anywhere where you can use Redux.

Rematch is less than 2 kilobytes in size, which means the impact on performance and the most important indicators for measuring that our website is going in the correct direction aren't affected.

The two key concepts when we analyze whether our page is responsive enough and sufficiently fast are as follows:

- **Time to Interactive (TTI)**: The time it takes for the website to be responsive
- **First Contentful Paint (FCP)**: The time once all the JavaScript has been downloaded and evaluated

We got the same results with Redux and Redux + Rematch on our Lighthouse suite, as shown in *Figure 4.1*. Lighthouse is an automated tool for improving the quality of web pages. It audits a lot of metrics, but we focused on performance:

Performance

Metrics

First Contentful Paint	0.2 s	Time to Interactive	0.2 s
Speed Index	0.2 s	Total Blocking Time	0 ms
Largest Contentful Paint	0.2 s	Cumulative Layout Shift	0

Figure 4.1 – Metrics of Lighthouse with Redux and Rematch

Now that we have seen that the performance of our website won't be affected by the bundle size of Rematch, let's take the first step of migrating to Rematch.

Migrating a Redux store to Rematch init

Redux's most relevant method is the `createStore()` method, as you'll remember from *Chapter 3, Redux First Steps – Creating a Simple To-Do App*, in the *Creating our first store* section, and is responsible for initializing our store and passing any additional configuration:

```
const store = window.Redux.createStore(
  reducer,
  window.__REDUX_DEVTOOLS_EXTENSION__ && window.__REDUX_
  DEVTOOLS_EXTENSION__()
);
```

`createStore()` doesn't exist in the Rematch library, being replaced instead by the `init()` function, which allows us to pass any Redux and Rematch configuration.

A best practice with Rematch is to think about the logic and split it inside models, but if our current application has too many reducers that can't be simplified or unified into single file models, it's a good practice to start with this simple step.

We're just using Rematch's `init()` function in the same way as `createStore()`:

```
const store = window.Rematch.init({
  redux: {
    reducers: {
      todos,
    },
  },
});
```

These snippets are equivalent and will work in the same way, but we want to simplify this even more.

We can replace the Redux property by just adding the following lines of code:

```
const store = window.Rematch.init({
    models: { todos }
});
```

But now, we must modify our reducers a bit more to become more familiar with the Rematch model.

Migrating Redux reducers to Rematch reducers

Rematch models contain a `state` property, a `reducers` property, and an `effects` property. We can use `state` to add the initial state, and inside `reducers`, we can move our Redux reducers directly to the reducers' `model` property:

```
const INITAL_STATE = {
  todos: []
}
function reducer(state = INITAL_STATE, action) {
  switch(action.type) {
    case "ADD_TODO": {
      const newTodo = {
        id: Date.now(),
        title: action.title,
        completed: false,
      }
      return {
        ...state,
        todos: [...state.todos, newTodo]
      }
    }"
    case "REMOVE_TASK": {
      const newTodos = state.todos.filter(todo =>
        todo.id !== action.id
      );
      return {...state, todos: newTodos }
    }
    case "TOGGLE_COMPLETED": {
      const newTodos = state.todos.map(todo =>
        todo.id === action.id ? { ...todo, completed: !todo.
        completed } : todo
      );
      return { ...state, todos: newTodos };
    }
    case "CLEAR_COMPLETED": {
      return INITAL_STATE
```

```
    }
    default: return state
  }
}
```

A common task when migrating to a Rematch model is removing the `switch` statements and instead using `state` or payload parameters on each reducer function:

```
const INITAL_STATE = {
  todos: []
}
const todos = {
  state: INITAL_STATE,
  reducers: {
    addTask: (state, title) => {
      const newTodo = {
        title,
        id: Date.now(),
        completed: false,
      }
      return {
        ...state,
        todos: [...state.todos, newTodo]
      }
    },
    removeTask: (state, id) => {
      const newTodos = state.todos.filter(todo => todo.id !==
      id);
      return {...state, todos: newTodos }
    },
    toggleCompleted: (state, id) => {
      const newTodos = state.todos.map(todo =>
        todo.id === id ? { ...todo, completed: !todo.completed
        } : todo
      );
      return { ...state, todos: newTodos };
    },
    clearCompleted: (state) => {
```

```
        const filteredTodos = state.todos.filter(todo => !todo.
        completed)
        return { ...state, todos: filteredTodos }
    }
  }
}
```

As you can see, the Rematch method is more readable because each reducer is just a pure function instead of a case inside a switch. Plus each reducer is automatically inferred with a first parameter, which is the global state, and the second parameter is an optional payload. This is very useful if we need to pass extra values for filtering and removing data.

With these changes, our application still won't work because we have changed the naming of our function reducers. We could decide to keep the reducer names the same as the switch statement names (ADD_TODO), instead of creating a reducer like this:

```
addTask: (state, title) => {
```

We could use the switch statement with double quotes:

```
"ADD_TODO": (state, title) => {
```

By keeping the reducer's name the same as the Redux application, instead of a simple camelCase function (addTask), the application will work as we expect from the beginning.

But in Rematch, we strongly recommend using simple camelCase functions for reducer names. In this way, everything becomes easier to maintain and to read.

In the next section, we'll see why Rematch recommends this naming convention and why it simplifies our code.

Migrating dispatch actions to effects

In our to-do app, we had four actions:

- Adding a task
- Removing a task
- Toggle completed
- Clear completed

Let's look at each one in more detail.

Adding a task

The following code snippet shows how to add a task to our store:

```
store.dispatch({
    type: "ADD_TODO",
    title: inputValue
});
```

With Rematch, this type of dispatch works out of the box, but it isn't recommended to use because it isn't type-safe and isn't very readable.

In Rematch, we adopt an alternative strategy of what Redux offers initially with the dispatch method. When Rematch initialises the store through the init() function or we add a new model using the store.addModel() function, we iterate over all the models and we create shortcuts for each reducer and effect for each model of our store. This means that we can access any reducer or effect of our store using direct access, such as an object. We recommend this method:

```
store.dispatch[MODEL_NAME][REDUCER_NAME|EFFECT_NAME](payload)
```

Taking the previous code snippet as an example, given a model name called todos and a reducer called ADD_TODO inside this model, we could execute the following:

```
store.dispatch.todos.ADD_TODO(inputValue)
```

This code snippet is equivalent to the previous code snippet with the store.dispatch({ type : "todos/ADD_TODO", title: inputValue }) method.

Removing a task and toggle completed

In *Chapter 3*, *Redux First Steps – Creating a Simple To-Do App*, in the *Dispatching actions* section, we created a function for unifying the logic of creating a button. We had four parameters. What if we can refactor this to just three parameters?

Our Redux code for creating generic buttons is as follows:

```
        createButton(task, "Remove", "REMOVE_TASK", todo.id);
        createButton(task, "Toggle done", "TOGGLE_COMPLETED", todo.
        id);
function createButton(parent, text, type, id) {
    const btn = document.createElement("button");
    btn.textContent = text;
```

```
  btn.addEventListener("click", () => store.dispatch({ type, id
  }));
  parent.appendChild(btn);
}
```

Now, just migrate it to Rematch dispatch callbacks:

```
    createButton(task, "Remove", () => store.dispatch.todos.
    removeTask(todo.id));
    createButton(task, "Toggle done", () => store.dispatch.
    todos.toggleCompleted(todo.id));
function createButton(parent, text, cb) {
  const btn = document.createElement("button");
  btn.textContent = text;
  btn.addEventListener("click", cb);
  parent.appendChild(btn);
}
```

We're just passing a third parameter as a new function that executes the reducer methods in the Rematch way of doing things. All this code is equivalent to the Redux code and works in the same way, but readability and maintainability are increased.

Clear completed

In our Redux application, we had this:

```
const clearTodosButton = document.getElementById("clear-
todos");
clearTodosButton.addEventListener("click", () =>
  store.dispatch({ type: "CLEAR_COMPLETED" })
);
```

Now, we just need to replace `store.dispatch()` with `store.dispatch.todos.clearCompleted()` because, as we saw in the previous section, in Rematch, we recommend using this shorthand:

```
const clearTodosButton = document.getElementById("clear-
todos");
clearTodosButton.addEventListener("click", () =>
  store.dispatch.todos.clearCompleted()
);
```

Now, everything should work as expected in our Redux application, but we have reduced tons of boilerplate if the application scales up in the future. We went from 100 lines of code to just 85 lines with the easiest implementation of Redux, but when our application needs to store data in a database or data needs to be persisted on a browser, things become complex and the Redux complexity increases drastically. But with Rematch, all this complexity can be easily handled via effects.

If we have our live server turned on, we can easily check that our functionality is back and that every functionality we developed with Redux works in the same way in Rematch:

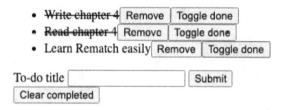

Figure 4.2 – Redux and Rematch example working

Now that we are proficient in migrating small Redux applications to Rematch, in *Chapter 5, React with Rematch – The Best Couple – Part I*, we'll see how to migrate asynchronous code from Redux to Rematch.

Summary

In this chapter, we learned the first steps of using Rematch and proved that Rematch reduces Redux complexity just by using pure functions and ES6 basic features. We also learned how to rename some methods, such as renaming createStore() to init(), and we covered migrating our Redux reducers from switch statements to Rematch reducers, which are easier to read and easier to maintain. We also migrated our dispatch actions from the dispatch({ }) Redux method to the Rematch shorthand.

In the next chapter, we will go deeper into a React and Rematch application with complex situations, such as listing products, creating a shopping cart, making calls to an external API, in summary, building a real-world web app with the best practices and performance.

Section 2: Building Real-World Web Apps with Rematch

On completion of this part, you will be able to create a shopping store website built with React, Tailwind, and Vite, where you'll be able to list products infinitely, add them to a shopping cart, and implement a search by product name feature. Also, you'll be able to test all these features with testing frameworks such as Jest and React Testing Library. You'll also learn which Rematch plugins can be added to this website and how they work internally.

In this section, we include the following chapters:

- *Chapter 5, React with Rematch – The Best Couple – Part I*
- *Chapter 6, React with Rematch – The Best Couple – Part II*
- *Chapter 7, Introducing Testing to Rematch*
- *Chapter 8, The Rematch Plugins Ecosystem*

5
React with Rematch – The Best Couple – Part I

In this chapter, we'll learn how to transform the client's requirements into mockups, create a user interface, list products inside an infinite scrolling list and add them to a shopping cart, and create a favorites system where the user can add products to a favorites list.

This chapter is one of the most important chapters in the book because it will serve as the basis for later chapters. We'll use the latest React technologies and features to start building the first prototype of our Amazon-like application.

In this chapter, we'll cover the following topics:

- Preparing the environment
- Creating the UI components

By the end of the chapter, you'll be able to create an application, create isolated components with a design system such as Tailwind, and explain how independent components come together in a real-world application.

Technical requirements

To follow along with this chapter, you will require the following:

- A basic knowledge of **Vanilla JavaScript** and **ES6** features
- A basic knowledge of **HTML5** features
- **Node.js >= 12** installed
- A basic knowledge of **React** and CSS (**TailwindCSS**)
- A browser (**Chrome**, **Firefox**)
- A code editor (for example, **Visual Studio Code**)

You can find the code for this chapter in the book's GitHub repository at `https://github.com/PacktPublishing/Redux-Made-Easy-with-Rematch/tree/main/packages/chapter-5`.

Preparing the environment

To get started with this chapter, we need to set up several things on our local machine, one of these being **Node.js**.

Node.js is a JavaScript runtime environment built on Chrome's V8 JavaScript engine, which comes bundled with a package manager called NPM. **NPM** is the world's largest software registry, and open source developers use NPM to share and borrow packages from each other.

The installation process for Node.js depends on your machine, so you can check the Node.js official website for official guidance: `https://nodejs.org`.

Once you have installed Node.js, we should be able to open a terminal and install **Yarn**. Yarn is an alternative to NPM, which is faster in several situations because it caches every package it downloads so that it never needs to do it again.

To install Yarn, just open a new terminal tab and run the following command:

```
npm install -g yarn
```

To check that the command ran correctly, run this command on the terminal:

```
yarn -version
```

You should see something like this: `1.22.10`.

Now we're ready to download the base application. In the previous chapters, we created our applications using UMD builds, but now we're going to use a no-bundler tool called **Vite**.

Vite is a no-bundler development environment that serves ES modules directly to the browser. Other options are available, such as webpack. With webpack, on each change, the code of our application must be re-bundled before shipping it to the browser. With Vite, our source code files are directly shipped to the browser as the browser requests them, letting the browser assume part of the role of a bundler, which means that we have a fast server start when developing our applications and, of course, faster updates.

To start our application, we'll scaffold a Vite and React project:

```
npx degit "PacktPublishing/Redux-Made-Easy-with-Rematch#create-
app-react-tw rematch-shop-app"
```

This command will create a folder called `rematch-shop-app` for us with all the necessary code to start developing our application. This is the basic scaffolding of a React single-page application website; you could use other alternatives that you are more comfortable with, such as Create-React-App, but it's recommended to follow the code suggested in the chapter so that you don't encounter strange errors that are hard to debug.

The file structure of our application should start like this:

```
├── api
│   └── db.json
├── index.html
├── package.json
├── postcss.config.js
├── src
│   ├── App.jsx
│   ├── index.css
│   └── main.jsx
├── tailwind.config.js
├── vite.config.js
└── yarn.lock
```

To get used to working with these files and for checking that `degit` downloaded our template correctly, you should check that these files exist:

- `api/db.json`: In this file, we introduced fake data to simulate the API of a store with products. We will use **json-server** (https://github.com/typicode/json-server), which automatically generates an API from a JSON file. When we run the `yarn dev` command, this will automatically start the API server on `http://localhost:8000` and the development environment where our website will reload on each change on `http://localhost:3000`, this is already preconfigured, you'll only need to run `yarn dev` to get started.

- `index.html`: This file includes the entry point of our application, in our case, `src/main.jsx`.

- `postcss.config.js`, `tailwind.config.js`: This file includes a configuration of our **Cascading Style Sheets** (**CSS**) framework called **Tailwind** (https://tailwindcss.com). This is not a requirement because we could write all the CSS manually, but using Tailwind utilities will help us to make the layout much easier. As you progress with the chapter, I will try to explain which CSS classes I'm using and why.

- `src/main.jsx`: This file only includes the required code from React to start an application.

- `Vite.config.js`: This is a configuration file provided by Vite to add plugins to our development server.

Now, we have to go inside this new folder, install all the dependencies, and start the project to check that everything is running fine:

```
cd ./rematch-shop-app
yarn install
yarn dev
```

We're just running `yarn install` to install all the dependencies, and `yarn dev` for running our development server, which will open a new tab on our browser at http://localhost:3000, where we should see the following screen:

Figure 5.1 – Amazhop running on our browser

As you can see, we have already set up some minimal layout to start our application, but what are the requirements of our application? They are as follows:

- We want to query a large list of products via infinite scroll. This means that we'll scroll through and the application will request more products when we archive the end of our scrolling container.
- We want to see whether a product is in stock.
- We want to add a product to the shopping cart.
- We want to see the total amount of the cart.
- We want to add products to a favorites list.
- We want to search/filter the products in the list by name.

Following all these requirements, we could draw a quick mockup of how our application will appear on the web:

Figure 5.2 – Amazhop mockup on the web

As we did in *Chapter 3*, *Redux First Steps – Creating a Simple To-Do App*, we have analyzed the requirements. We have designed a quick mockup and we're ready to build the user interface components step by step.

In the next section, we'll start on the building blocks that will make our application beautiful in terms of design but refrain from adding any logic yet.

Creating the user interface components

To start building the user interface, we should decide which components will be necessary, looking at the mockup we proposed.

We can see that we have a lot of components, so let's separate the bigger ones from the smaller ones:

- Header
- Product List
- Cart

These are the biggest ones, so let's go step by step.

Header

To create a Header component, let's start by creating a folder in our /src directory. This will be /components folder where we'll store all our components.

Then we'll create a Header.jsx file inside the /components directory with this content:

```
import React from "react";


export const Header = () => (
  <div className="grid grid-cols-0/5 grid-rows-1 bg-gray-900
  p-3 gap-3 items-center">
    <h1 className="text-white text-3xl font-extrabold tracking-
    tight underline">
      Ama<span className="bg-clip-text text-transparent bg-
      gradient-to-l from-purple-400 to-pink-200">zhop</span>
    </h1>
    <input type="text" className="p-2 rounded-md"
    placeholder="Search products..." />
  </div>
);
```

In this file, we're creating a simple grid layout for splitting our logo to the left and the input to the right.

With this component created, we must add it to the `App.jsx` file to be injected into our application:

```
import { Header } from "./components/Header";
```

This will import our `Header` component, and we're ready to use it on our `App` component:

```
const App = () => {
  return (
    <div className="w-full max-w-8xl mx-auto min-h-screen">
      <Header />
```

If we have been running our development server, we should have seen an automatic refresh of our browser with the header rendered on our application. If you have to turn it on, just run `yarn dev` and access `http://localhost:3000`.

Now, we should see our website header with our logo and the search box:

Figure 5.3 – Amazhop preview with the Header component

As you can see, the search box still doesn't search anything. Throughout the chapter, we'll discover how to implement this feature and how Rematch does this filtering really easily.

Now, let's analyze the `Product List` component.

Product List

The `Product List` component is a bit more complex than the `Header` component because we have individual product items. Our plan is to create an infinite scroll component, so it's recommended to extract the list to one component and the item to another component.

Let's start creating a new folder in our /components folder, called ProductList, and inside this, a List.jsx component, a Product.jsx component, and an index.jsx file.

I like to create an index.jsx file for component folders that contain multiple components. This helps us to export all the components that are in that folder in a single import instead of two.

Now, let's get started with the List component, which will be the wrapper of our Products components.

List component

For now, our List component is really simple: just a <div> element to give it a background color and some padding, and then the layout with a grid:

```jsx
import React from "react";

export const List = () => {
  return (
    <div className="bg-gray-100 p-3">
      <div role="list" className="grid grid-cols-2 xl:grid-cols-3 2xl:grid-cols-4 3xl:grid-cols-5 gap-8 2xl:gap-5 3xl:gap-5">
        Product list
      </div>
    </div>
  );
};
```

The List component will be responsible for connecting to the Redux store and rendering all the product's components, but right now we're just focusing on creating the user interface.

With the List component ready, we must create the products of our list.

Product component

For our project, we must create a layout for our `Product` component cards similar to this:

Figure 5.4 – Product card mockup

We can see that we'll require the following:

- A card wrapper:

```
<div role="listitem" className="w-auto border rounded-md
shadow-sm bg-white flex flex-col">
```

- A product image:

```
<img loading="lazy" src="https://via.placeholder.com/150"
className="w-full rounded-t" />
```

- The product name, whether the product is in stock, the price of the product, and a brief description of the product:

```
<div className="flex-grow p-6">
    <h1 className="text-xl font-semibold">Product
    name</h1>
    <div className="text-xl font-medium text-gray-
    500">Product price</div>
    <div className="w-full text-sm font-medium
    text-green-500 mt-2">Product stock</div>
    <div className="text-sm text-gray-400">
        Product description
    </div>
</div>
```

- Two buttons, one for making a purchase and one for adding it to favorites:

```
<div className="flex space-x-3 mb-4 text-sm font-semibold
px-6">
  <div className="flex-auto flex space-x-3">
    <button className="w-full flex items-center
    justify-center rounded-md bg-gray-900 text-white
    disabled:opacity-50 disabled:cursor-not-allowed"
    type="button">Add to cart</button>
  </div>
  <button className="flex-none flex items-center
  justify-center w--9 h-9 rounded-md text-gray-400 border
  border-gray-300" type="button" aria-label="like">
    <svg width-"20" height-"20" fill-"currentColor">
    <path fillRule="evenodd" clipRule="evenodd"
    d="M3.172 5.172a4 4 0 015.656 0L10 6.34311.172-
    1.171a4 4 0 115.656 5.656L10 17.6571-6.828-6.829a4
    4 0 010-5.656z" />
    </svg>
  </button>
</div>
```

All these HTML elements could be extracted to separate components, such as the buttons, but each application has its requirements, so you'll have to tell by the mockups and the client requirements whether it's worthwhile to extract those components to be reused. In our case, to keep it simple, we decided not to extract them.

Now we should export these components to index.jsx to facilitate an easier importing into other files of our application:

```
export { List } from "./List";
export { Product } from "./Product";
```

Let's import the Product component into our List component, which will be responsible for rendering and connecting to the Redux store:

```
import { Product } from ".";
```

Next, import the Product component into the List component, and then we're ready to replace Product list line with some Products:

```
<div role="list" className="grid sm:grid-cols-2 md:grid-
cols-2...">
  <Product />
  <Product />
</div>
```

We're rendering two products inside our List component because when we set up Rematch, all these products will come from the API and will be rendered dynamically. Now, we're just creating the user interface. We must add our List component to App.jsx, as we did on previous occasions:

```
...
import { List } from "./components/ProductList";

const App = () => {
    return (
        <div className="w-full max-w-8xl mx-auto min-h-
        screen">
            <Header />
            <div className="grid sm:grid-cols-1 md:grid-
            cols-0/5 grid-rows-1 min-h-screen">
                <List />
            </div>
        </div>
    );
};
```

To check that our components are rendered properly, we should see something like the following in our development environment, as shown in *Figure 5.5*:

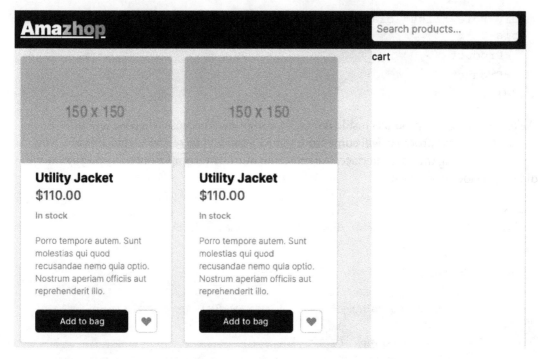

Figure 5.5 – Amazhop with the Product List and Header components

All these components are built using Tailwind for the styling, so it's recommended to check the Tailwind website to understand the `classNames` strings that we're using. They're pretty straightforward because their names match the styles. To give you an example, `w-full` is equal to a width of `100%` (*width full*), and `p-3` is equal to a padding of `12px`. If you decide to build this website without using Tailwind, you can recreate our own CSS stylesheets following the Tailwind classes, but we strongly recommend using Tailwind for focusing on Rematch and not the style/design.

Now we can start building the last component, `Cart`.

Cart component

The Cart component contains two components, the cart itself and CartProduct. This component is responsible for showing the product information of every product that appears in the shopping cart, and it will also handle the units added to the cart of every product. As we did in the ProductList cart, let's create a folder called Cart inside the /components folder, with three files – index.jsx, Cart.jsx, and CartProduct.jsx:

```
export const Cart = () => {
  return (
    <div className="bg-white border shadow-sm divide-y sticky
    top-0 h-screen pt-16 overflow-y-auto">
      <header className="p-3 flex justify-between items-
      center">
        <div>
          <h3 className="font-medium text-lg">Your cart
          total:</h3>
          <span aria-label="total cart">$1000.00</span>
        </div>
        <button type="button" className="rounded-md p-2 bg-
        gray-900 text-white">
          Clear
        </button>
      </header>
      <div role="list" className="divide-y divide-gray-100">
        cart
      </div>
    </div>
  );
};
```

The Cart component will be responsible for rendering CartProduct and will also handle the cart total and the clear button, which will clear out the entire cart.

With `Cart` ready, let's now create the `CartProduct` component, which will be rendered inside the `Cart` component:

```
export const CartProduct = () => {
  return (
    <article role="listitem" className="p-4 flex space-x-4">
      <img
        src="https://via.placeholder.com/150"
        alt="Product image"
        loading="lazy"
        className="flex-none w-auto max-w-16 max-h-16 rounded-
        lg object-cover bg-gray-100"
      />
      <div className="flex-auto">
        <h2 className="text-lg font-semibold text-black under">
          Utility Jacket
        </h2>
        <p className="text-sm font-medium text-gray-500">
          $110.00
        </p>
      </div>
      <div className="flex items-center">
        <button className="w-5 h-5 rounded-md text-gray-400
        border border-gray-300 mr-2" type="button" aria-
        label="remove">
          <svg xmlns="http://www.w3.org/2000/svg" fill="none"
          viewBox="0 0 24 24" stroke="currentColor">
            <path strokeLinecap="round" strokeLinejoin="round"
            strokeWidth="2" d="M18 12H6" />
          </svg>
        </button>
        <div aria-label="product quantity" className="w-auto
        p-2 h-7 text-sm flex items-center justify-center
        rounded-md text-gray-500 border border-gray-300 mr-2">
          0
        </div>
        <button className="w-5 h-5 rounded-md text-gray-400
        border border-gray-300 mr-2" type="button" aria-
        label="purchase more">
```

```
            <svg xmlns="http://www.w3.org/2000/svg" fill="none"
            viewBox="0 0 24 24" stroke="currentColor">
                <path strokeLinecap="round" strokeLinejoin="round"
                strokeWidth="2" d="M12 6v6m0 0v6m0-6h6m-6 0H6" />
            </svg>
          </button>
        </div>
      </article>
   );
};
```

This component is an alternative to the Product component, because instead of being vertical, it is horizontal but will be filled with similar product information. It also includes two buttons for increasing or decreasing the units purchased of that product.

With these two components ready, we must export them to the index.jsx file:

```
export { Cart } from "./Cart";
export { CartProduct } from "./CartProduct";
```

Now, we can import the Cart component inside our App file:

```
import { Cart } from "./components/Cart";
```

We can also replace our previous cart code, which looks like this:

```
<div>
    cart
</div>
```

And replace it with our new Cart component:

```
<Cart />
```

And now we're ready to add hypothetical cart articles to our cart to check that the design is rendered correctly:

```
import { CartProduct } from "./";
```

Add this import to Cart.jsx and then render some products in the cart:

```
<div role="list" className="divide-y divide-gray-100">
    <CartProduct />
```

```
<CartProduct />
<CartProduct />
</div>
```

Now that we're done with our user interface, we already have all the components that we'll need to build our application, so let's check the final result by accessing our development environment:

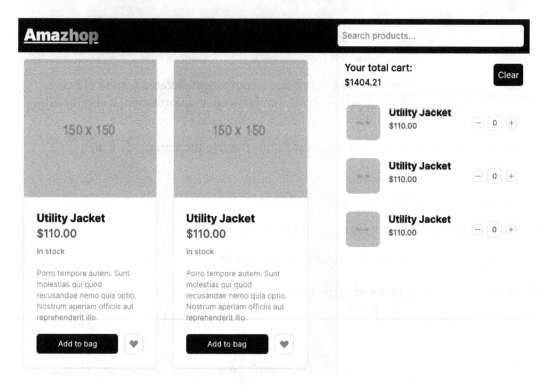

Figure 5.6 – Amazhop final result with all the components rendered

Our application is cool, pretty, and responsive… but right now it doesn't do anything, it's just HTML elements with some CSS classes, so what's pending? Now we have to include side effects, or, to put it better, asynchronous operations, because our products will come from an API. This situation is where Redux developers suffer and code complexity jumps up several notches.

In the next chapter, we're going to see which methods are available to request from this API, how are we going to request them, and how Rematch encapsulates all this logic in independent files practically out of the box.

Summary

In this chapter, we have learned how to prepare the environment to create an application and how we can transform requirements into something visible through mockups and bring things to life with React, Also we learned how to use a CSS framework such as Tailwind for styling our React components, and how we can split our code into components to maintain code that is cleaner and safer to use.

In the next chapter, we'll learn how to create business logic with Rematch for these components and see how React and Rematch fit perfectly for designing a long-term application that can be maintained and improved over time.

6
React with Rematch – The Best Couple – Part II

In this chapter, we'll complete the work that we started in the previous chapter, where we analyzed the mockups and transformed those requirements into a complete web shop application using Tailwind and React, but the application didn't have any interactivity. In this chapter, we'll be able to list products within an infinite scrolling list calling to an external API, add them to a shopping cart, and create a favorite system where the user can add products to a favorites list.

In this chapter, we'll cover the following topics:

- Creating the shop business logic
- Binding components with business logic

By the end of the chapter, you'll be able to create any application with side effects, call any API remotely, and treat this data to create business logic and inject it into isolated components with a design system such as Tailwind. We'll see how we can build our application to production mode and how independent components come together in a real-world application.

Technical requirements

To follow along with this chapter, you will need the following:

- Basic knowledge of **vanilla JavaScript** and **ES6** features
- Basic knowledge of **HTML5** features
- **Node.js >= 12** installed
- Basic knowledge of **React** and CSS
- A browser (**Chrome** or **Firefox**)
- A code editor (for example, **Visual Studio Code**)

You can find the code for this chapter in the book's GitHub repository at `https://github.com/PacktPublishing/Redux-Made-Easy-with-Rematch/tree/main/packages/chapter-6`.

Creating the shop business logic

As we explained in *Chapter 5, React with Rematch – The Best Couple – Part I*, in the *Preparing the environment* section, we're using an interesting NPM module named `json-server` (`https://github.com/typicode/json-server`) that converts static **JavaScript Object Notation** (**JSON**) files to API endpoints ready to use. This module is really powerful for this book because it will allow us to call a fake API to access the data. A real API recovers the data from a database, but in our case, this data is just static. However, the way this data is accessed from our side, on the frontend, is the same as would be employed in a real API.

When we start our application with `yarn dev`, it automatically runs a server on `http://localhost:3000` to see the refreshed changes of our frontend application, while also running a server on `http://localhost:8000`. If we access this URL, we should see something like this:

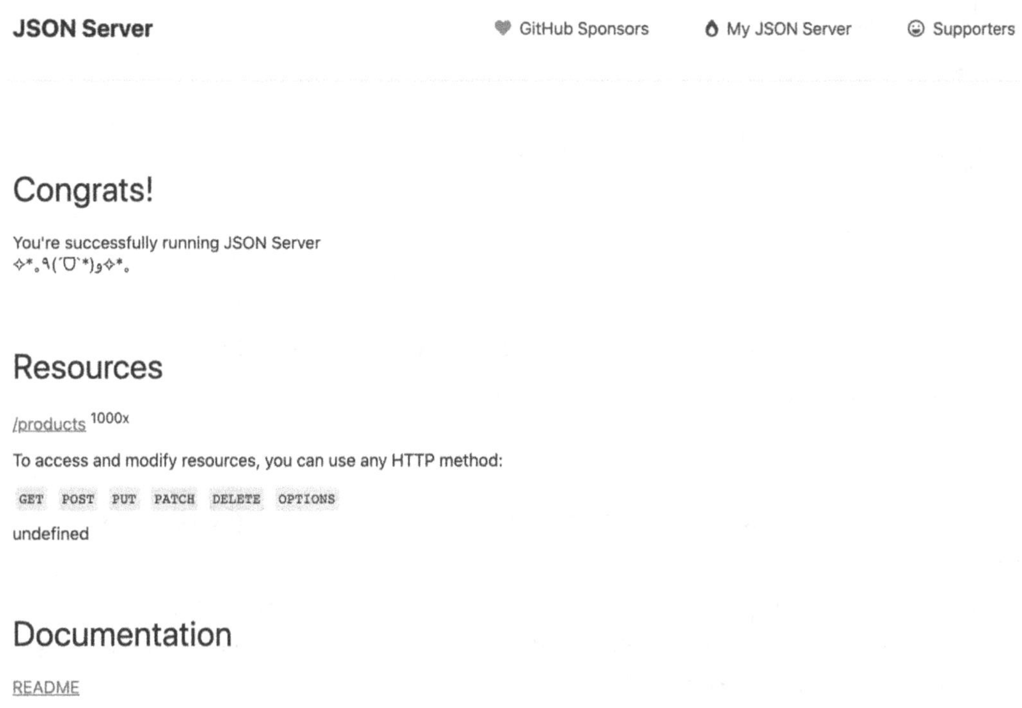

JSON Server   ♥ GitHub Sponsors   ◊ My JSON Server   ☺ Supporters

Congrats!

You're successfully running JSON Server
✧*｡٩(ˊᵕˋ*)و✧*｡

Resources

/products ¹⁰⁰⁰ˣ

To access and modify resources, you can use any HTTP method:

`GET  POST  PUT  PATCH  DELETE  OPTIONS`

undefined

Documentation

README

Figure 6.1 – JSON server local website accessing localhost:8000

If you want to know more about this module, you can click on the **README** link in the **Documentation** section and you will see in detail how it works and which methods are exposed to the API.

To check that everything is running smoothly and our API is returning data, we can use **cURL** in our terminal to check that we have results.

Copy and paste this into your terminal and then press *Enter*:

```
curl "http://localhost:8000/products?_limit=1"
```

cURL is a tool integrated into practically every machine that transfers data. In our case, we're requesting the data served from the `json-server` module via cURL, limiting the result to just one product.

You should see something like this:

```
[→ ~ curl 'http://localhost:8000/products?_limit=1'
[
  {
    "id": "41fd4fd9-95c7-4809-96db-a147d352fdbb",
    "image_url": "https://dummyimage.com/400x400/28200e/000&text=Unbranded Metal Chair",
    "stock": 8,
    "productName": "Unbranded Metal Chair",
    "price": 43,
    "productDescription": "Porro tempore autem. Sunt molestias qui quod recusandae nemo quia optio. Nostrum aperiam officii
s aut reprehenderit illo.",
    "favorite": false
  }
]
→ ~
```

Figure 6.2 – JSON server returning the data we requested via cURL

To start this section, we need to install some dependencies:

```
yarn add react-redux redux @rematch/core
```

These dependencies are the basic ones to get started with any Rematch project. Let's split them:

- react-redux: This is the official library of Redux for using Redux hooks with React. When we install Rematch with Redux in React projects, probably 99% of the time we will also need to install the react-redux package.

- redux: This is the Redux module.

- @rematch/core: This is the official Rematch package. It comes with everything we need to start developing our application.

With these dependencies installed, we're ready to create a Rematch store. Let's create a folder inside src/ called /store with an index.js file inside it:

```
import { init } from "@rematch/core";
export const store = init({});
export dispatch = store.dispatch;
```

As in *Chapter 4, From Redux to Rematch – Migrating a To-Do App to Rematch,* in the *Migrating the Redux store* section, we're initializing the Rematch store without models yet, so let's first create the /models folder inside the /store folder, and here we'll create three files – cart.js, shop.js, and index.js. Our shop and cart files will contain all the business logic of our application; they are basically objects with state, reducer, and effect properties, as we explained in *Chapter 2, Why Rematch over Redux? An Introduction to Rematch Architecture,* in the *How does Rematch work?* section.

The shop Rematch model file content is as follows:

```
export const shop = {
  state: {},
  reducers: {},
  effects: {}
};
```

The cart Rematch model file content is as follows:

```
export const cart = {
  state: {},
  reducers: {},
  effects: {}
};
```

They are empty Rematch models, as you'll remember from the previous chapters.

Now we have to export them for further use. The index.js file must export both as a single import:

```
export { shop } from "./shop";
export { cart } from "./cart";
```

Now, we can import the /src/store/models/index.js file into the /src/store/index.js init() function:

```
import { init } from "@rematch/core";
import { shop, cart } from "./models";

const models = { shop, cart };

export const store = init({ models });
```

As you can see, this strategy is the same for any implementation of Rematch on any framework. We performed these steps in the Redux vanilla application in *Chapter 4, From Redux to Rematch – Migrating a To-Do App to Rematch*, in the *Migrating the Redux store* section, and we're doing the same steps in this React application. This means that we could create a totally framework-agnostic layer of business logic, meaning that it could be used in any framework and will work practically out of the box by just changing a few minor details. If you followed *Chapter 3, Redux First Steps – Creating a Simple To-Do App*, in the *Creating our first store* section, you will have installed the Redux DevTools extension in your browser and you may have noticed that the icon of the extension turned from gray to green when we imported the Rematch store file inside the `main.jsx` file:

```
import { store } from "./store";
```

To make sure that Redux DevTools extension is running correctly in our website you should see the icon as shown in *Figure 6.3* in your browser bar:

Figure 6.3 – Redux DevTools extension in standby mode

Why does the extension turn green? Because our `init()` function is doing the internal setup of Redux, the DevTools option works out of the box, and the models are correctly initialized with empty objects in our Rematch store.

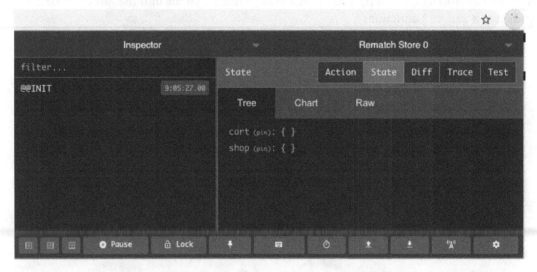

Figure 6.4 – Redux DevTools running when adding the import store inside the main.jsx file

Alright, we have our Rematch store initialized but... how do we subscribe to listen to changes that have occurred in our Rematch store? With the `store.subscribe()` method, right? In part, yes, you can, but it isn't recommended.

When using Redux together with React, the recommended approach is to use the `react-redux` library. This library comes with React components to make things easier. You wrap your entire application with the `Provider` component, and you pass a prop store with the Rematch store instance, and this component will be responsible for making the Rematch store available to any nested component that needs to access this store.

Let's apply this definition to our application inside `main.jsx`:

```
...
import { Provider } from "react-redux";
import { store } from "./store";

ReactDOM.render(
  <React.StrictMode>
    <Provider store={store}>
      <App />
    </Provider>
  </React.StrictMode>,
    document.getElementById("root")
);
```

As you can see in the highlighted code, we're wrapping our entire application with the `Provider` component, passing a store prop, which is our Rematch store returned from the `init()` function. This will make the Rematch store accessible from any component inside our provider.

If we don't want to use the `react-redux` `Provider` method, we would have to use `store.subscribe()` manually in every component. This is standard behavior when writing a vanilla application with Redux, but since we're using React, we can take advantage of the benefits that React has as a framework.

With this concept clear in our minds, we're ready to start making requests to our API service, but how can we use the cURL method in the browser? There's a native method called **Fetch**. The Fetch API provides an interface for fetching resources in the same way as cURL does, but it's usable in many browsers. Almost all browsers, except Internet Explorer 11, are compatible with this method. The `fetch()` method, which exposes this interface, takes one mandatory argument, the path to the resource you want to fetch, and it returns a Promise that resolves the response to that request, irrespective of whether it's successful.

Using the example involving the cURL method that we used a few pages back, we have the following:

```
curl "http://localhost:8000/products?_limit=1"
```

We can write an equivalent using the `fetch()` method:

```
const data = await fetch('http://localhost:8000/products?_
limit=1');
const result = await data.json();
```

The first line is doing a GET request to the resource path passed as an argument, and the second line is parsing the response to JSON. JSON is a standard text-based format for representing structured data based on JavaScript object syntax.

If we execute these two lines in our browser using the `Inspect` tool, for example, we can check that the response result is the same for the cURL method and `fetch()`.

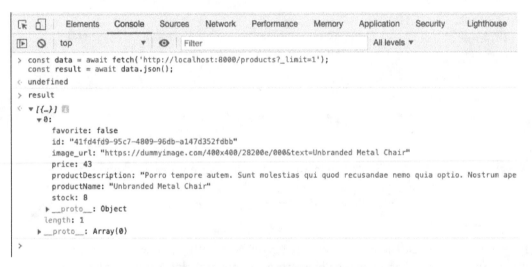

Figure 6.5 – Inspect tool example of the fetch() method

But we don't stop here. There are other alternatives that are even easier for making requests to API services. Imagine doing API requests in just one line, cancelable requests, client-side support for protecting against XSRF, intercept and transform requests and responses – all these features in just 13.5 kilobytes. That's what **Axios** offers (https://github.com/axios/axios).

Following the previous example using `fetch()`, we can migrate it to use Axios instead:

```
await axios.get('http://localhost:8000/products?_limit=1');
```

As simple as that, we won't need `data.json()` anymore because Axios automatically transforms the response into JSON data.

But what if we can use the same API that Axios exposes in less than 1/5th of the size of Axios? This is where **Redaxios** comes in. Redaxios is made using the browser's native Fetch API, but creates a little wrapper around Fetch for cloning the Axios API. Instead of having to choose between Axios and Fetch, Redaxios provides a middle ground between the two.

We're going to use Redaxios in our project because his simplicity and small foot-print in our bundle size, but you could use native Fetch API or Axios or any wrapper for making asynchronous requests easier, so let's install Redaxios:

```
yarn add redaxios
```

Now, let's create a folder called `/utils` inside our `/src` directory. Inside the `utils` folder, we'll create a file called `apiClient.js`.

`apiClient.js` will contain a little class to make calling our API methods even easier:

```javascript
import Http from "redaxios";
const isReactNative = typeof navigator !== "undefined" &&
navigator.product === "ReactNative";

class ApiClient {
  constructor() {
    this.httpInstance = Http.create({
      baseURL: isReactNative ? "http://10.0.2.2:8000" :
      "http://localhost:8000",
    });
  }

  async get(url, params) {
    return this.httpInstance.get(url, { params });
  }

  async patch(url, body, params) {
    return this.httpInstance.patch(url, body, { params });
  }
};

export default ApiClient;
```

We are storing a Redaxios instance inside our `ApiClient` class using the `Http.create()` method with a `baseURL` property. This is helpful for not having to write the same URL in every request, which could result in an error if we write the URL incorrectly. Instead, if we write the URL just once, we won't fail.

Also, we expose a `get` method for passing parameters as a second argument instead of passing an object with a `params` property. This is useful for increasing readability because our URL parameters will be automatically encoded from an object to a valid URL with parameters.

With this file created, we're ready to inject this `ApiClient` class inside our models to request data to our API client. To get started with Rematch asynchronous requests we can start by adding the effect that will be responsible of fetching products from our API.

getProducts()

The `getProducts` effect will be responsible of requesting products 10 by 10 each time we reach the bottom of our website and adding them to the shop state.

Let's start by importing our `ApiClient` utility at the top of the `/store/models/shop.js` file:

```
import ApiClient from "../../utils/apiClient";
const api = new ApiClient();
```

Now, we should ask ourselves which state will contain our shop model. We should store some products, and also we should know what's the current page of our API. This is usually used to manage pagination or in our case requesting products 10 by 10 every time we reach the bottom.

So, let's add that property to the shop model state:

```
const api = new ApiClient();
export const shop = {
  state: {
    products: [],
    currentPage: 1,
    totalCount: 0,
  },
```

We decided that our shop model will be initialized with an empty array of `products`, a `currentPage` property initialized to 1, and a `totalCount` number, which will be the total products that will return our API service. It will be useful to know when to stop requesting data when we have already requested all the data.

Now, we should write our `getProduct()` effect and its corresponding reducer to add the data to the store. Always remember that the store won't be added to the model state if you don't execute the reducer. Effects, by themselves, never introduce data into the state:

```
effects: () => ({
  async getProducts(_, { shop }) {
    const { currentPage } = shop;
    const { data, headers } = await api.get("/products", {
      _page: currentPage,
      _limit: 10,
    });
    const totalCount = parseInt(headers.get("x-total-
count"));
    this.SET_PRODUCTS({ products: data , totalCount });
  }
```

The `getProduct()` effect is an async method that doesn't have any payload, which is why we're using an underscore for that parameter, and we're using a second parameter, also known as the `RootState` parameter, which contains the entire state of our application.

We're using it to get the current page to be able to paginate the results. There are several ways of handling this logic, with one of them being storing the current page in the Rematch state in such a way that it can be accessed from anywhere (imagine a pagination component that can change this value), or can also be handled with a local state, using `React.useState()`, and passing `currentPage` through the payload (the first parameter).

When the request is resolved, we call `this.SET_PRODUCTS(data)`. Why this?

```
reducers: {
  SET_PRODUCTS(state, { products, totalCount }) {
    return {
      products: [...state.products, ...products],
      currentPage: state.currentPage + 1,
      totalCount: totalCount,
    };
  }
},
```

The `this` method is filled by Rematch with any reducer and effect method that is in the same model. For example, taking the current implementation, we could use `this.getProducts()` or `this.SET_PRODUCTS()`.

This is equivalent to `dispatch.[modelName]`, in our case, `dispatch.shop`.

If we run `console.log` function of `dispatch.shop` and the `this` object, this produces the following output:

```
console.log(dispatch.shop);
console.log(this);
```

To demonstrate that `dispatch.shop` and `this` object are equivalent, see the `console.log` printing in our browser:

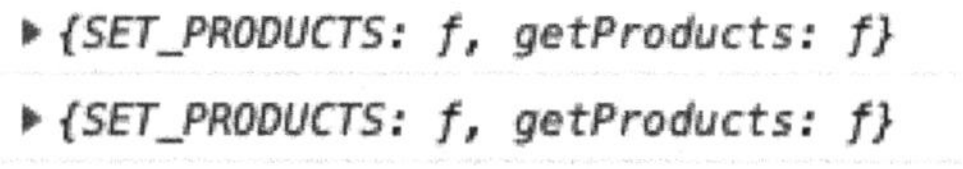

▶ *{SET_PRODUCTS: f, getProducts: f}*
▶ *{SET_PRODUCTS: f, getProducts: f}*

Figure 6.6 – An equivalent demonstration of dispatch.shop and this

The benefit of `dispatch` is that you can execute any reducer or any effects of any model of your store, unlike `this`, which can only run self-context methods.

In terms of explaining the code, why would we call the reducer in uppercase and snake case format? This is a personal recommendation. I've been developing applications with Redux and Rematch for some years, and I always find it interesting to differentiate easily which method is a reducer and which method is an effect. I like to write effect names in camel case (writing phrases without spaces and indicating the separation of words with a single capitalized letter) and write reducers in snake case (separating words with an underscore):

```
SET_PRODUCTS(state, { products, totalCount }) {
    return {
      products: [...state.products, ...products],
      currentPage: state.currentPage + 1,
      totalCount,
    };
  }
```

So, taking our reducer code, we are just merging the actual state products with the new products coming from the `getProduct` effect (the second parameter), increasing `currentPage` on each request and passing `totalCount` for later use in the user interface.

With the shop model ready to be injected into the user interface, first, we're going to implement the cart logic and focus on adding this logic to the view in the next section, *Binding components with business logic*.

Which methods should be required in cart business logic? Adding a product to the cart, removing products from the cart, and clearing the cart to its initial state.

The initial state of our cart could be a list of products and a total sum of the products' prices for each quantity added to the cart. But why would we duplicate the products array in the cart model when we already have this information in the shop model? The recommended approach for every Redux application is to normalize the data, but what does this mean?

- Each type of data gets its own model in the state.
- Each model should store the individual items in an object, with the IDs of the items as keys and the items themselves as the values.
- Any references to individual items should be done by storing the item's ID, instead of referencing the whole item.
- Arrays of IDs should be used to indicate ordering.

Taking our application as an example, we should create a cart state with this schema:

```
state: {
    addedIds: [],
    quantityById: {}
},
```

`addedIds` will include all the product IDs added to the cart, and `quantityById` will contain an object with the same length of keys as `addedIds`, which will be the product ID as a key and the number of products added to the cart as the value.

Following this definition, we could have a state with the following information:

```
state: {
    addedIds: [
        "some-id",
        "other-id"
    ],
    quantityById: {
        "some-id": 1,
```

```
    "other-id": 4
  }
},
```

This code snippet could be an example of a real cart model, some IDs, and their corresponding quantities.

With everything we already know, should we use effects or reducers to handle this logic? Reducers, of course, as effects are only recommended for use when we need to include side effects, and our cart business logic is just pure functions, removing, pushing, and spreading data. There aren't any side effects.

Adding products to the cart

As we saw previously, I personally like to name reducers with uppercase and snake case format; so, following this recommendation, we get the following output:

```
reducers: {
    ADD_TO_CART(state, product) {
        const indexProduct = state.addedIds.indexOf(product.id);
        if (indexProduct === -1) {
            return {
                addedIds: [...state.addedIds, product.id],
                quantityById: {
                    ...state.quantityById,
                    [product.id]: 1,
                }
            };
        }

        return {
            addedIds: state.addedIds,
            quantityById: {
                ...state.quantityById,
                [product.id]: (state.quantityById[product.id] || 0) +
                    1
            }
        };
    }
```

In these 20 lines of code, we're handling the real behavior of adding products to a cart. When adding a product to a shopping cart, we could already have that product in the cart, which is why the first line does `.indexOf(product.id)` to check whether we already have that product in our `addedIds` array.

If the product is already in the cart, we must change the `quantityById` object, but instead of just initializing the value to `1`, as in the first section of the code, we increment the current state value by `1`. This is useful for increasing the quantity in the cart or purchasing the same product several times.

Removing products from the cart

As we did in the previous section, we must check that our product is in our shopping cart, but in this case, we don't need to add an extra step when the product isn't in the cart (because we can't remove something that isn't there), which is why we do an early return of the current state if `.indexOf` is equal to `-1` (which means that the ID hasn't been found):

```
REMOVE_FROM_CART(state, product) {
    const indexProduct = state.addedIds.indexOf(product.id);
    if (indexProduct === -1) return state;

    const clonedIds = [...state.addedIds];
    const clonedQuantityById = state.quantityById;
    if (clonedQuantityById[product.id] === 1) {
      clonedIds.splice(indexProduct, 1);
      delete clonedQuantityById[product.id];
    } else {
      clonedQuantityById[product.id]--;
    }
    return {
      addedIds: clonedIds,
      quantityById: clonedQuantityById
    };
  },
```

Why do we need to clone `state.addedIds` and `state.quantityById`? Redux requires all reducer logic to be written using immutable updates, so to change any value inside the store, you need to return a new reference of the state.

Our code is basically checking whether the current quantity of the product is passed as an argument. It is equal to 1, which means that we should entirely remove the ID from the addedIds array and delete the key-value property from the quantityById object.

If it isn't equal to 1, for example, it's 2 or 3, this will just decrease the quantity value.

Restoring the cart to its initial state

This method is the easiest one because it's just returning the desired initial state, in our case, just an empty array for addedIds, and an empty object for quantityById:

```
RESTORE_CART() {
    return {
        addedIds: [],
        quantityById: {},
    };
    }
```

We could create a constant value to make sure that RESTORE_CART() returns the same value that we wrote in the state property of our model:

```
const INITIAL_STATE = {
  addedIds: [],
  quantityById: {}
};
export const cart = {
  state: INITIAL_STATE,
  reducers: {
    RESTORE_CART() {
      return INITIAL_STATE;
    },
```

This code is self-explanatory, just a constant value that contains our state, and we share the constant variable in our model's initial state and our RESTORE_CART reducer.

Now, we have the basic logic to make our application work as a real application, but how can we trigger these effects and these reducers? In the next section, we'll see how we can use React life cycles to trigger our effects and how we can use the react-redux library to access our state.

Binding components with business logic

In this section, we're going to explore how all this logic we've introduced can be injected inside our React application, using React hooks. Hooks are a new addition to React 16.8. They let you use the state and other React features without writing a class. This is the recommended approach of developing components with React since we often have problems with maintaining components that started out simple but have grown into an unmanageable mess of stateful logic and side effects, becoming, all in all, unmaintainable. If you don't know how hooks work, reading this official React guide should be the first step: `https://reactjs.org/docs/hooks-intro.html`.

The `react-redux` library includes its own custom hook APIs, which allow your React component to subscribe to the Redux store and also to the Rematch stores. Rematch is 100% compatible with the `react-redux` library and works out of the box with its API, making any migration from Redux to Rematch even easier.

As you will recall, in *Chapter 3, Redux First Steps – Creating a Simple To-Do App*, in the *Dispatching actions* section, we saw a function called `store.getState()`, which returned us the whole state of our application, but in React, we can benefit from the `react-redux` API using a new hook called `useSelector()`:

```
const products = useSelector(rootState => rootState.shop.
products)
```

This code is an example of recovering the products array from our shop model. `rootState` means that we have access to any state of our store. In terms of the result, it is equivalent to calling `store.getState().shop.products`.

The `useSelector()` hook allows you to extract data from the Redux store state, using a selector function. You may be wondering why we don't use the `store.getState()` function directly, and that's a good question because it looks similar and more or less does the same thing, returning a state value, but there are some differences:

- The `useSelector()` hook internally uses the `store.getState()` function, but it benefits from the React API, using techniques such as strict reference comparisons with the last result, so if the last result strictly equals the new value, the component will not re-render; it's like a little cache that improves our website performance with zero effort.

- It accepts an equality function as a second argument, which means that we could introduce a different technique of caching. Instead of checking the value as a strict reference comparison (===), we could use a shallow comparison for more aggressive caching.

All these techniques couldn't be done using just `store.getState()`. That is why the default approach for using React and Rematch/Redux involves the use of hooks.

Let's start by connecting our `List` component, which is situated in this folder: `/src/components/ProductList/List.jsx`.

Connecting the product list

The `List` component, by definition, has to deal with the situation when our Rematch effect has to be called. We will also use the `useSelector()` hook to recover the products and `totalCount`.

Let's start by taking the requirement we defined for this component:

"We'll be able to list products inside an infinite scrolling list calling to an external API."

What does that mean, **infinite scrolling list**? Infinite scrolling is a web design technique that loads content continuously as the user scrolls down the page. This entirely removes the need for pagination controls. A good example of how this works is social media sites such as Twitter, Facebook, and Instagram.

To use this feature in React, we can benefit from hooks and install a tiny dependency called `react-infinite-scroll-hook` (`https://github.com/onderonur/react-infinite-scroll-hook`). This hook basically expects three properties:

- `loading`: When `true`, this property won't load more content because it's still loading the current content.
- `hasNextPage`: When `false`, this property means that we don't have more items to recover from our API, so more content won't be loaded.
- `onLoadMore`: This property expects the function to be called when the user reaches the sentry. Basically, we'll have an element of the DOM that will be a reference for this library to be aware of when more content has to be loaded.

To install it, we just need to run the following command:

```
yarn add react-infinite-scroll-hook
```

Once it's installed, we'll import the hook inside our `List.jsx` component to be used later:

```
import useInfiniteScroll from "react-infinite-scroll-hook";
```

Recovering data from the useSelector hook

To create a subscription with the store and recover the data when we dispatch actions, we can import the `useSelector` hook:

```
import React from "react";
import { useSelector } from "react-redux";

export const List = () => {
  const { products, totalCount } = useSelector(rootState =>
  rootState.shop);
  console.log({ products, totalCount });
```

We can check that `products` and `totalCount` return our Rematch shop model's initial state because we're returning the selector function, `rootState.shop`.

Now, we can dispatch an action, our previously created `getProducts()` effect. We just need to import the `useDispatch` hook that the `react-redux` package offers:

```
import { useDispatch } from "react-redux";
```

In our case, we're going to dispatch the `getProducts()` effect inside the `useEffect()` hook.

The `useEffect()` hook is a hook written by React that lets you write side effects in function components. If you're familiar with React class life cycle methods, the `useEffect` hook is similar to a mix of `componentDidMount`, `componentDidUpdate`, and `componentWillUnmount`:

```
import React, { useEffect } from "react";
import { useSelector, useDispatch } from "react-redux";

import { dispatch } from "../../store";

export const List = () => {
  const { products, totalCount } = useSelector(rootState =>
  rootState.shop);
  const dispatch = useDispatch();
  console.log({ products, totalCount });
```

```
useEffect(() => {
  dispatch.shop.getProducts();
}, []);
```

This code is importing the `dispatch` method exported from our store and executing the `getProducts()` method inside the shop model when the component is mounted because the `useEffect()` hook will run and clean it up only once (on mount and unmount) because we passed an empty array, `[]`, as a second argument. This tells React that your effect doesn't depend on any values from props or state, so it never needs to be re-run.

If we check the console, we can see that `console.log` has been logged two times, once with an empty `products` array, and now with the first 10 products, and that `totalCount` is 1000:

```
▼ {products: Array(0), totalCount: 0} 🔘                                    List.jsx:8
  ▶ products: []
    totalCount: 0
  ▶ __proto__: Object
▼ {products: Array(10), totalCount: 1000} 🔢                                List.jsx:8
  ▶ products: (10) [{…}, {…}, {…}, {…}, {…}, {…}, {…}, {…}, {…}, {…}]
    totalCount: 1000
  ▶ __proto__: Object
```

Figure 6.7 – Demonstration of console.log logging the shop state

With our first 10 products already in our state, we can start to render them using the `.map()` function, and import our `Product` component that we created previously:

```
import { Product } from "./Product";
```

This code is importing the `Product` component inside our `List` component. This component will contain two props, the key, which is mandatory in the case of React when using the `.map()` function, and a `product` prop for passing the product information:

```
<div role="list" className="grid grid-cols-2 xl:grid-cols-3
2xl:grid-cols-4 3xl:grid-cols-5 gap-8 2xl:gap-5 3xl:gap-5">
      {products.map((product) => (
        <Product
          key={product.id}
          product={product}
        />
      ))}
</div>
```

In this code, we're just mapping the products array and passing to our Product component the product information pertaining to each one.

Now, we should see something like this, but… every product contains the same information, right? That's because we designed our application with static data but now, we're receiving dynamic data from an external API and passing this data individually to every Product component, so we have to tweak our Product component slightly to read the product information from the product prop:

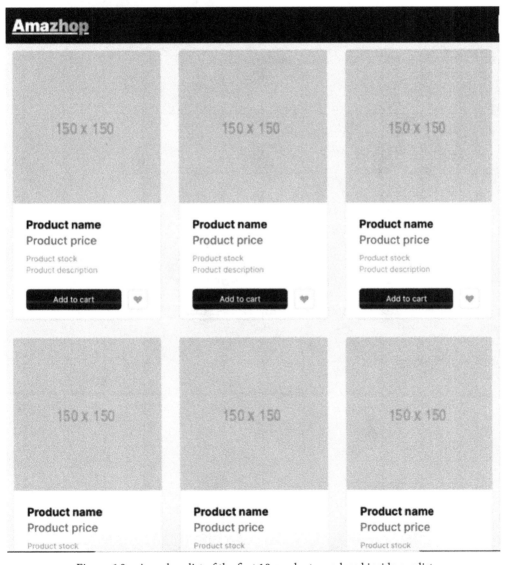

Figure 6.8 – Amazhop list of the first 10 products rendered inside our list

As you know, React props are accessible via `this.props` if it's a class component or the first parameter in the case of function components. In our case, we wrote all our components like functions, so to be able to print the product information dynamically, we should extract the product prop from the first argument of our component. We can benefit from **ES6** features and use the destructuring technique to destructure every prop passed to the `Product` component:

```
export const Product = ({ product }) => {
```

Here, we're destructuring the props argument and receiving information relating to every product that we have inside our Rematch shop state.

As you'll remember, our `Product` schema looks like this:

```
{
    "id": "41fd4fd9-95c7-4809-96db-a147d352fdbb",
    "image_url": "... ",
    "stock": 8,
    "productName": "Unbranded Metal Chair",
    "price": 43,
    "productDescription": "P.",
    "favorite": false
},
```

Now, our image code inside our `Product` component will be rewritten as follows:

```
<img loading="lazy" src={product.image_url} className="w-full
rounded-t" />
```

The product name is as follows:

```
<h1 className="text-xl font-semibold">
    {product.productName}
</h1>
```

The product price is as follows:

```
<div className="text-xl font-medium text-gray-500">
    {number(product.price)}
</div>
```

What is the number function? I've decided to create a file inside src/utils/ formatters.js with some interesting formatters for our website, so instead of showing just **43**, we're showing **$43.00**. This is possible thanks to an official Internationalization API that provides locale-sensitive functions. This means that by giving a locale, for example, **en-US**, we'll get the corresponding date, number, or plurals with the language-specific rules for that locale.

The content of our formatters.js file will be a number function that formats any number to a USD currency:

```
const nF = new Intl.NumberFormat("en-US", { style: "currency",
currency: "USD" });
export const number = (number) => nF.format(number);
```

Now, you can use this function anywhere in your application and format any number to a more human-readable number.

Returning to what we were doing, let's continue with the product stock:

```
export const Product = ({ product }) => {
const hasStock = product.stock > 0;
    return (
```

Since we're going to use this value in more sites, we can save this ternary expression of checking whether the product stock is higher than 0, which means that we have stock of this product. We're going to store this Boolean indicator inside the hasStock constant.

Now, we must install a tiny utility called clsx (https://github.com/lukeed/clsx). This is for constructing className strings; conditionally, it's just 228B:

```
yarn add clsx
```

Import the utility as follows:

```
import clsx from "clsx";
```

Now, we have modified our `className` property with the `clsx()` function, which has a ternary operator. Remember that a ternary operator is an `if` statement inline. In our case, it's just checking whether we have stock, and if so it must return the `"text-green-500"` class, and if we don't have stock, it must return the `"text-red-500"` class:

```
<div className={clsx("w-full text-sm font-medium mt-2",
hasStock ? "text-green-500" : "text-red-500")}>
  {hasStock ? "In stock" : "No stock"}
</div>
```

Also, in the child of the `div` element, we're doing a similar expression, but instead of returning classes, we're returning a simple string indicating whether the product is **In stock** or **No stock**.

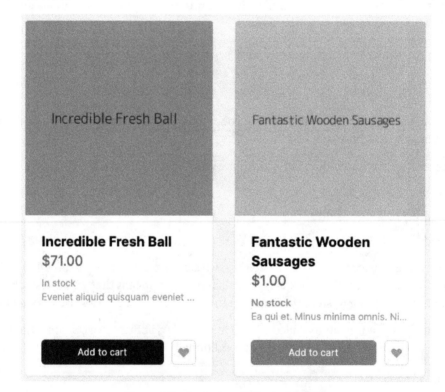

Figure 6.9 – In stock and No stock labels

The product description is as follows:

```
<div className="text-sm text-gray-400 overflow-ellipsis
overflow-hidden truncate ...">
    {product.productDescription}
</div>
```

It is as simple as replacing the static information and adding the reference to our product prop.

The **Add to cart** button is as follows:

```
<button disabled={!hasStock} className="w-full flex items-
center justify-center rounded-md disabled:opacity-50
disabled:cursor-not-allowed bg-gray-900 text-white"
type="button">
    Add to cart
</button>
```

The **Add to cart** button benefits from the hasStock constant we defined previously, and we're disabling this button if we don't have any stock of the product.

The product favorite/heart icon button is as follows:

```
<button type="button" aria-label="like"
    className={clsx("flex-none flex items-center
    justify-center w--9 h-9 rounded-md border border-gray-300",
    product.favorite ? "text-red-500" : "text-gray-400"
)}>
```

In the favorite button, we use the clsx utility and a ternary expression to change the heart color from gray to red when the favorite is true.

Now, we have finished our `Product` component and we should see our product list looking like this:

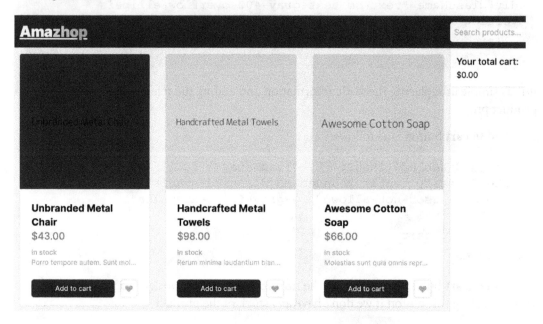

Figure 6.10 – Amazhop with dynamic data and images

Our products are correctly rendered dynamically, and the prices are formatted correctly.

What's happening right now? We are scrolling, but the page doesn't render more items, and that's because we haven't implemented this feature yet.

In the next section, we're going to conclude the implementation of the infinite scrolling list that we'll be able to scroll, and automatically our application will load products ten by ten everytime we reach the bottom of our website.

Loading more items on scroll

To get started with this section, we're using a dependency that must be installed. If you haven't installed it yet, install `react-infinite-scroll-hook` using `yarn` and import it inside the `List` file:

```
import useInfiniteScroll from "react-infinite-scroll-hook";
```

Now, we're going to modify our `List` component to initialize the infinite scroll hook:

```
export const List = () => {
    const { products, totalCount } = useSelector(rootState =>
    rootState.shop);
    const hasNextPage = totalCount > products.length;
    const [infiniteRef] = useInfiniteScroll({
        loading: false,
        hasNextPage,
        onLoadMore: () => dispatch.shop.getProducts(),
    });
```

In this code snippet, we're adding a new constant called `hasNextPage`, which will also be used inside `return()` of the function. Basically, it's checking that `totalCount` (which we know is `1000` because our API returns the total number of products that we have in `db.json`) is greater than the length of the current product from our Rematch store. Meanwhile, if the length of our product is less than `1000`, we'll request more items.

Also, we're initializing `useInfiniteScroll` with a property called `onLoadMore()`, which calls our API via the global dispatch. As we explained previously, the infinite scroll hook works thanks to an official API called Intersection Observer, which provides a way to track the actual visibility of a target element as a human being would define it. Basically, it allows us to create elements that are still not visible but when they are, we get notified.

This means that we have to add a sentry element to notify Intersection Observer that we must load more items because we have reached the bottom:

```
{products.map(product => (
  <Product
      key={product.id}
      product={product}
  />
))}
{hasNextPage && <div ref={infiniteRef}>Loading...</div>}
```

The sentry element can be anything you want. In our case, we decided to add an indicator of loading, but it could be an empty `div` element, a spinner animation, or even an image.

With these changes applied, we should check that our list where we're scrolling is fully functional and we're requesting products ten by ten every time we arrive at the bottom of the products list, making it fast and accessible.

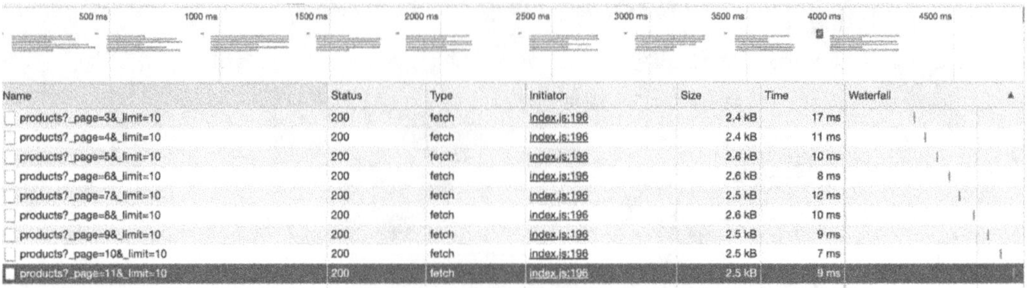

Name	Status	Type	Initiator	Size	Time	Waterfall	▲
products?_page=3&_limit=10	200	fetch	index.js:196	2.4 kB	17 ms		
products?_page=4&_limit=10	200	fetch	index.js:196	2.4 kB	11 ms		
products?_page=5&_limit=10	200	fetch	index.js:196	2.6 kB	10 ms		
products?_page=6&_limit=10	200	fetch	index.js:196	2.6 kB	8 ms		
products?_page=7&_limit=10	200	fetch	index.js:196	2.5 kB	12 ms		
products?_page=8&_limit=10	200	fetch	index.js:196	2.6 kB	10 ms		
products?_page=9&_limit=10	200	fetch	index.js:196	2.5 kB	9 ms		
products?_page=10&_limit=10	200	fetch	index.js:196	2.5 kB	7 ms		
products?_page=11&_limit=10	200	fetch	index.js:196	2.5 kB	9 ms		

Figure 6.11 – The network inspect tool tab showing the different requests made when we scrolled

Now, we must go further with our application since we tried to click on the **Add to cart** button but nothing happened.

In the next section, we're going to connect our cart model with our Cart component, and we'll build some utility functions that will help us to make the useSelector hook more readable in complex scenarios.

Connecting our application to the Cart logic

Since we have already seen how the useSelector hook works, we'll be faster in this step, so let's get started.

Inside the src/components/Cart/Cart.jsx component, we must import the useSelector hook:

```
import { useSelector } from "react-redux";
```

Then, inside our component, we'll recover the two main values of our cart model:

```
const { addedIds, quantityById } = useSelector(rootState =>
rootState.cart);
```

Here, we're recovering the addedIds array and the quantityById object. We'll use them to calculate the total price of our cart and which products we must render inside the cart list.

Mapping addedIds to the products schema

To map `addedIds` to products, basically we have to iterate over this ID and replace the ID by the corresponding product in the shop model. To do this, we can also use the `useSelector` hook:

```
const cartProducts = useSelector(rootState => addedIds.map(id
=> getProduct(rootState, id)));
```

In this code snippet, we are taking the `addedIds` value and using the `.map()` function with a `getProduct(rootState, id)` function, but what is the `getProduct` function? Inside our cart model, we can expose any function that could be useful to us or could be reused. In our case, we're going to create the `getProduct` and `getQuantity` functions:

```
export const getProduct = (state, id) => state.shop.products.
find(product => product.id === id);
export const getQuantity = (state, id) => state.cart.
quantityById[id];
```

The `getProduct` function basically takes the `rootState` object of our application, accessing the shop model and searching any product where the ID matches the ID passed to the function.

The `getQuantity` function is accessing the cart state and recovering the number of products we want to purchase given an ID.

Mapping quantityById to the total price cart

To get the total price of our cart, this basically requires a simple reducer function. We must iterate over all the products that we have in our cart, and for each product, we must get the price and multiply this price by the quantity we added to the cart:

```
const totalPrice = useSelector(rootState => addedIds.reduce(
        (total, id) => total + getProduct(rootState, id).price *
        getQuantity(rootState, id),
    0
));
```

This code snippet uses the `.reduce()` function, which is a method that executes a reducer function on each element of the array, resulting in a single output value. In our case, we're summing to a total variable that is initialized to zero, the sum of the current total plus the product price multiplied by the quantity.

With all these constants ready, we can introduce the `onClick` function, which will be triggered when we click the **Add to cart** button.

We must import inside our `Product` component, situated in `/src/components/ProductList/Product.jsx`:

```
import { dispatch } from "../../store";
```

Then, we have to modify our **Add to cart** button to trigger the `dispatch` function when the user clicks on it:

```
<button … onClick={() => dispatch.cart.ADD_TO_CART(product)}>
   Add to cart
</button>
```

With this change, we can check that we can click on the button and Redux DevTools logs a new action, our `cart/ADD_TO_CART` reducer.

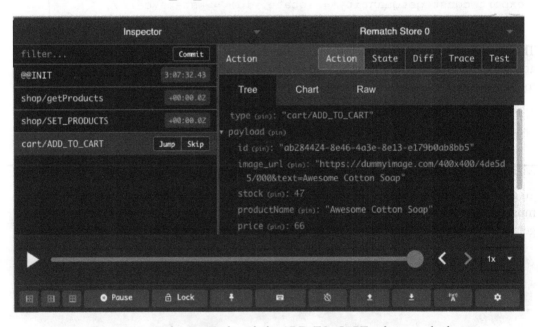

Figure 6.12 – Redux DevTools with the ADD_TO_CART reducer method

Our cart state contains products, but these aren't rendered yet. That's because we need to modify our `Cart` component slightly to render `cartProducts` dynamically:

```
<div role="list" className="divide-y divide-gray-100">
    {cartProducts.length ? cartProducts.map(product => (
    <CartProduct key={product.id} product={product}
    quantity={quantityById[product.id]} />
    )) : (
        <div className="text-center">
            <h5 className="font-medium text-lg pt-6">Empty
            cart</h5>
        </div>
    )}
</div>
```

We're passing to `CartProduct` the product information via props, but also, we're passing the quantity we purchased. Since this property is in our store and will be repainted every time, we dispatch an action that changes the state of the cart.

Now, we must modify our `CartProduct` component to render and dispatch actions as we did with the `Product` component:

```
<img
        src={product.image_url}
        alt="Product image"
        loading="lazy"
        className="flex-none w--auto max-w-16 max-h-16
        rounded-lg object-cover bg-gray-100"
    />
    <div className="flex-auto">
        <h2 className="text-lg font--semibold text-black under">
            {product.productName}
        </h2>
        <p className="text-sm font-medium text-gray-500">
            {number(product.price)}
        </p>
    </div>
```

In this code snippet, we're just replacing the static information we used for designing this component and we're referencing the product information coming from the component props.

With these changes, we can check that adding a product to the cart gets painted correctly.

Figure 6.13 – CartProduct rendered inside the Cart component

But the quantity doesn't change and our minus and plus buttons don't change our amount, so let's fix this.

We must modify the buttons as we did in the **Add to cart** button, adding an `onClick` event handler:

```
<button onClick={() => dispatch.cart.REMOVE_FROM_CART(product)}
```

This one is for removing the product from the cart, as you may remember what the logic was. If the quantity is higher than 1, we'll decrease the quantity from our `quantityById` object. If not, we remove that item from both properties.

Now we must modify the plus button, to increase the amount:

```
<button onClick={() => dispatch.cart.ADD_TO_CART(product)}
```

Also, we have to replace our static 0 with the `quantity` prop:

```
export const CartProduct = ({ product, quantity }) => {
```

We use the destructuring pattern to extract the `quantity` property coming from the Cart component:

```
<div aria-label="product quantity" className="w-auto p-2 h-7
text-sm flex items-center justify-center rounded-md text-
gray-500 border border-gray-300 mr-2">
{quantity}
</div>
```

We render the quantity value, and now, if we add some products to the cart, we will see that our cart is 100% functional.

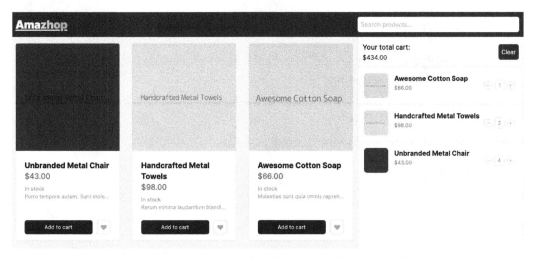

Figure 6.14 – The cart and product lists rendered correctly

Restoring the cart to an empty state

Restoring the cart to an empty state is really easy since we've added a reducer method called RESTORE_CART inside our cart model.

We just need to modify the src/components/Cart/Cart.jsx file and add an onClick handler to the **Clear** button:

```
<button onClick={() => dispatch.cart.RESTORE_CART()}
```

We can check that clicking on this button makes the cart return to its empty state.

Introducing the search feature

There are multiple ways of handling this type of feature, with the most common being to pass a query parameter to our API service and the results will come already filtered, and then we just need to replace our products array with the new array provided by our API.

Since this method is really common and simple, I've decided to go with something a bit more complex:

1. The user will write anything in the search bar and won't implement a search until the *Enter* key is pressed.

2. The user query will be saved in our store.

3. Then, the user query stored in our store will be used to filter our data locally, which means that we're going to filter the products inside our model.

4. The user can reset to the initial state by clicking on the reset button or just removing the query and pressing *Enter* again.

Let's start by modifying the shop model to store the query requested by the user, for posterior use in the `Cart` component.

Modifying the shop model

In our shop model, we just need to introduce a new reducer, called `SET_QUERY`:

```
SET_QUERY(state, query) {
    return {
        ...state,
        query,
    };
}
```

This reducer returns the entire state and adds a new property called `query`, which is passed from the payload parameter.

Introducing Header logic

Now, our `Header` component must control what the user is writing:

```
import React, { useState } from "react";
import { useDispatch } from "react-redux";

export const Header = () => {
    const dispatch = useDispatch();
    const [value, setValue] = useState("");
```

`useState` is a React hook. Basically, it declares a state variable. `useState` is a new way to use the exact same capabilities that `this.state` provides in a class. Normal constants or variables defined in a function component disappear when the component unmounts, but the state variables are preserved by React.

We're using this variable to store the value that the user is writing in the input:

```
<input
        onChange={(e) => setValue(e.target.value)}
        value={value}
        type="text"
        className="p-2 rounded-md w-full"
        placeholder="Search products..."
    />
```

Basically, we're passing from an uncontrolled input to a controlled one. This means that we're controlling via the `value` property the value that the input must contain instead of the default DOM value attribute.

Now, we have to add an event handler to detect when the user presses the *Enter* key. This is done via the `onKeyPress` event, which returns an event that contains a key, in our case, `"Enter"`:

```
onKeyPress={(e) => {
            if (e.key === "Enter") {
                dispatch.shop.SET_QUERY(e.target.value !== "" &&
                e.target.value);
            }
        }}
```

In this code, we're dispatching the `SET_QUERY` method when the user presses the *Enter* key. If the value is an empty string, we return `false`, and this will be useful for restoring the initial state.

Now we're ready to include a button inside our input text to reset the query filtering:

```
<div className="relative">
        <span className="absolute inset-y-0 right-0 flex
        items-center pr-2">
            <button
                onClick={() => {
                    dispatch.shop.SET_QUERY(undefined);
                    setValue("");
                }}
                type="button"
```

```
            className="text-sm shadow-sm p-1 bg-gradient-to-l
            from-purple-400 to-pink-200 rounded-lg text-white"
    >
            Reset
        </button>
    </span>
    <input
```

When the onClick event occurs, this button will basically execute the SET_QUERY dispatcher with a false value, and also runs the setValue() function without any value. This will reset the input value to undefined.

Alright, our input text is now functional, but the products aren't filtered yet, so let's modify our List.jsx file:

```
import { filterByName } from "../../store/models/shop";

export const List = () => {
  const query = useSelector(rootState => rootState.shop.query);
  const products = useSelector(rootState => query ?
  filterByName(rootState, query) : rootState.shop.products);
```

In this code snippet, we're importing the filterByName function, which is basically .includes(), and using it inside useSelector of the product's constant. If the user has introduced any query to the store, the products selector will filter the products by name; if the query is false, this selector will return the products without filtering.

Our filterByName function looks like this:

```
export const filterByName = (rootState, query) => {
  return rootState.shop.products.filter((product) => {
    return product.productName.toLowerCase().includes
    (query.toLowerCase());
  });
};
```

We're using a simple .filter() function to the shop products array with toLowerCase() when comparing the strings to provide a full case insensitive text search feature.

When we're returning the products filtered, we don't want an infinite scroll, because when filtering the products, we're just filtering with the current products of our store, so let's modify our infinite scroll sentry to only render when a query is not present:

```
{hasNextPage && !query && <div ref={infiniteRef}>Loading…</
div>}
```

We can write a product title inside the `SearchBox` component to check that correctly filters products by their name:

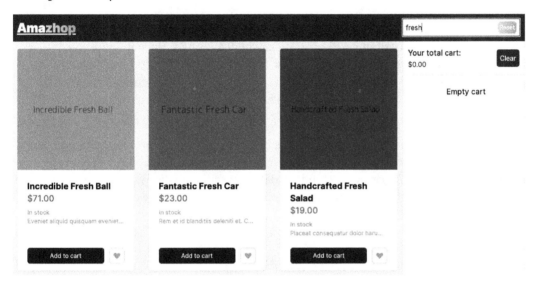

Figure 6.15 – Demonstration of search box filtering by "fresh"

As you can see, we filtered our products correctly with the word `fresh`. Even when written as capitalized, `Fresh` is being filtered. Now, there's just one feature left to implement – adding products to favorites.

Adding to favorites

This feature is really easy since the `json-server` API lets us make patch requests given an ID.

In our shop model, we just need to add a new effect and a new reducer:

```
async setToFavorite({ id }, rootState) {
  const productIndex = rootState.shop.products.findIndex(
    (el) => el.id === id
  );
```

```
   if (productIndex === -1) return;
   const product = rootState.shop.products[productIndex];
   const { data } = await api.patch(`/products/${id}`, {
     favorite: !product.favorite,
   });
   this.SET_FAVORITE({ indexToModify: productIndex, product:
   data });
 },
```

This effect, called `setToFavorite`, expects an object with an ID. The ID will be used to establish what resource of our API must be patched/modified. Since in our effects we also have access to the `rootState` parameter, we can find which resource needs to be patched. If it isn't in our store, we do an early return; if it's in our products array, we use the opposite favorite value, so basically dispatching this effect will toggle whether it's a favorite or not.

Once the API returns that the resource has been modified correctly, we must pass the data to the reducer to modify this resource from our product's state. This could be resolved again by calling the `getProducts()` effect and recovering the data from the API with the updated changes, but since we're just updating a single property, we can perform the following logic:

```
 SET_FAVORITE(state, { indexToModify, product }) {
   const products = [...state.products];
   products[indexToModify] = product;
   return {
     ...state,
     products,
   };
 },
```

We use the index previously found in the effect to modify the copy of our shop products, and then, as always, we return the new state reference.

Alright, we already have the logic, but now we need to modify our `Product` component to dispatch this effect when clicking on the heart button:

```
       <button
         onClick={() => dispatch.shop.setToFavorite({
           id: product.id,
         })}
```

With this code, we're dispatching the `setToFavorite` effect with the `id` property. Automatically, when we click this button, the list will be repainted with the heart button turning red or gray.

To check that everything is working, I selected the first two products from my favorites list and, as you can see, the heart is red in the case of the first two products, while the third is gray:

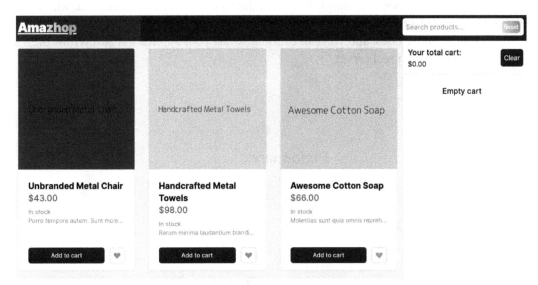

Figure 6.16 – The favorite feature working as expected, showing two red hearts

Our application is finished, and everything is working smoothly, but there's one pending task: building it to a production environment using the `yarn build` command:

```
yarn build
yarn serve
```

The `yarn build` command runs the Vite bundler in production mode. This command will generate a folder called `/dist`, which could be used to deploy this application to any hosting provider. Since it's a single-page application without any routing or server-side techniques, that is why we could deploy it easily to any hosting provider since these are just static files:

```
$ vite build
vite v2.1.5 building for production...
✓ 75 modules transformed.
dist/index.html                0.63kb
```

```
dist/assets/index.2e5909d9.css    7.57kb / brotli: 2.21kb
dist/assets/index.9a207491.js     8.44kb / brotli: 2.75kb
dist/assets/vendor.5da409ad.js    147.55kb / brotli: 41.79kb
```

Our entire website is less than 170 kilobytes, with all the dependencies bundled and ready to be served to the browser.

If we run the `yarn serve` command, this starts the `vite preview` command, which basically starts an HTTP server in the `http://localhost:5000` URL, similar to what a hosting provider does, and you can check how fast your application is and how the application will load on a real server.

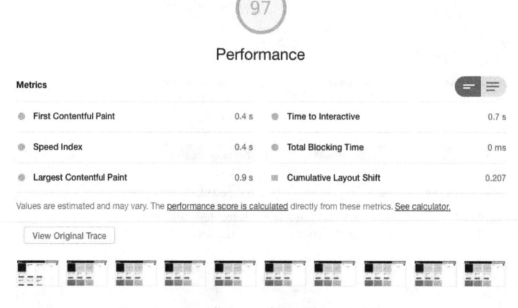

Figure 6.17 – A performance of 97 on Chrome Lighthouse

Our application is fast and small, has been bundled in less than 4 seconds, and is totally functional. The user can list products, add them to the shopping cart, decrease and increase the product quantity in the cart, format the numbers for a given locale, and filter by name and add to favorites, but there are a lot of new features that can be added to this website that we'll see in the chapters that follow.

We'll see in the next chapter how this application becomes a rock with a full suite of tests including unit testing for our Rematch models and integration testing for our React views with models. We'll analyze how React testing works and how Rematch models can be injected into our tests to simulate end user behavior.

Summary

In this chapter, we have learned how to create an amazing, complete, Amazon-like application. We have also learned how Rematch affects work in real API requests, how we can design, analyze, and start developing some client requirements, and, most importantly, how Rematch architecture makes developing any application easy and predictable.

Now, we'll be able to create any application with Rematch and React with side effects, including carrying out the first steps of analyzing our clients' requirements, converting them to mockups, and then creating our application without any business logic with just styles, and then adding the layer of business logic and connecting this logic to the components. We also saw how to build an application to a single-page application and test Lighthouse performance, and what our application looks like in production mode.

In the next chapter, we'll learn how to integrate Jest and the React Testing Library in this application. We will execute a test by unit testing the Rematch models to avoid regressions in our business logic, and we'll also use the Testing Library to test the user interface.

7
Introducing Testing to Rematch

In this chapter, we'll learn how to correctly test a real application using the best practices and the latest technologies out there. We'll learn about the differences between different types of testing and how our application can be easily refactored if our testing suite covers enough code to give us the confidence to move pieces of code without breaking the functionality.

This chapter is important to understanding testing concepts and the different libraries for testing. Also, it's important for understanding how Rematch models can be tested and learning about different concepts such as `rootReducers` that haven't been covered yet.

In this chapter, we'll cover the following topics:

- Introduction to JavaScript testing
- Preparing the environment
- Creating tests for Rematch models
- Creating tests for React components

By the end of the chapter, you will have learned what types of JavaScript testing exist nowadays and how they evolved to develop applications with confidence. Also, you'll learn how to properly set up these tools and how Rematch's models and React components can be tested together or independently. Also, you'll learn which metrics of testing are interesting and useful for our application.

Technical requirements

To follow along with this chapter, you will need the following:

- Basic knowledge of vanilla JavaScript and ES6 features
- Basic knowledge of HTML5 features
- Node.js >– 12
- Basic knowledge of React and CSS
- A browser (Chrome or Firefox, for instance)
- A code editor (Visual Studio Code, for instance)

You can find the code for this chapter in the book's GitHub repository: `https://github.com/PacktPublishing/Redux-Made-Easy-with-Rematch/tree/main/packages/chapter-7`.

Introduction to JavaScript testing

A couple of years ago, JavaScript testing was really obfuscated because no one used to care about testing front-end websites. HTML and CSS were not tested – no one even thought to test it – and JavaScript testing was strange to see. One of the main problems was that a lot of developers were coming from Java, where JUnit introduced everything needed to test an application – a test runner, a library to write the tests, an assertion library – and no equivalents existed for JavaScript.

We had to install three libraries to do something similar for JUnit. That meant that we had to learn how these three libraries worked, and of course there were situations where testing some edge cases was impossible due to incompatibility between libraries.

Let's start understanding how testing now works in JavaScript.

Types of tests

To understand how testing works a bit more and what types of testing exist, I'll try to explain in a few lines the three principal types of tests that exist nowadays and some terminology that is used in this chapter that is essential to know:

- **Unit tests**, as the name indicates, test parts of our application individually, which means testing whether a function, module, or class that receives X input returns Y value. These tests run in isolation and independently of each other, giving us extra confidence in parts of our application that could tend to fail.

- Even if our entire application is unit tested, it will still mean that parts of our application are not being tested together. **Integration tests** try to combine all the modules, dependencies, and functions and test how they work together. Thanks to these tests, we can make sure that our application will work correctly as a whole.

- **End-to-end tests** let us test our application in a real browser environment. The point of these tests is to simulate an actual user within our application. When using these types of tests, we can simulate behaviors such as clicking on elements, typing inputs, and checking whether everything is rendered correctly from the point of view of an actual user.

Test frameworks

To be able to introduce any of these testing methodologies, we'll benefit from interesting frameworks such as **Jest**, which is a JavaScript testing framework maintained by Facebook. It works practically out of the box with any project written in React, Angular, Svelte, or Vue.js.

Jest exposes some global functions, called **matchers**, that let us compare easily what type or which value to expect:

```
test('two plus two is four', () => {
  expect(2 + 2).toBe(4);
});
```

This test is expecting that 2+2 will equal 4. There are tons of matchers and they can be extended easily through other libraries such as **Testing Library**.

Testing Library is a testing utility built to test the **Document Object Model (DOM)** tree rendered by React on the browser, letting us write tests that resemble how a user would use our application. Instead of running these tests on a real browser, Jest offers a solution that is called **JS-DOM** that lets Jest render any component to a virtual browser that can be queried later with the utility functions that Testing Library exposes. To understand this concept a bit more, imagine a scenario where we have a button for the user with the text **Buy!**. React's Testing Library can expose a utility called `screen.getByText("Buy!")` that will return us the DOM element associated with that text. If it's found, it will imply that our application is rendered correctly and as a consequence, the user will see that button in the browser.

Throughout the chapter, I'll explain which queries we're using and how they work.

Mocking in tests

Mocking functions allow us to test the links between code by erasing the actual implementation of a module and returning a new implementation. To be clear, it's for overwriting implementations of our source code in our tests by keeping the source code with the original implementation.

Mocking in the past was used to mock side effect operations. We mocked what our API was returning by mocking the `fetch()` interface or the custom library that we were using.

Instead of mocking all these `fetch()` functions, a new generation of mocking for API appeared called **Mock Service Worker (MSW)**.

These mocks are based on intercepting requests at the network level instead of the implementation level, which is super cool because if we decide to change our internal implementation of how our API requests are done, these tests will still work, and we won't need to change anything in our tests because it doesn't touch the implementation details.

We'll configure the MSW library later in the chapter, and we'll explain in a bit more depth how this library works and how it handles the requests done by our application.

Coverage

Testing coverage is a metric used to measure the amount of source code tested by our testing suite. Coverage will find areas of our code that are not covered by any test case, which means that increasing the coverage value will directly increase the quality of our testing suite.

In this chapter, we'll try to achieve 100% coverage of our application and see how Jest handles this out of the box with an amazing report and detailed analysis.

In the next section, we'll introduce the new dev dependencies required to make Jest work and how they're configured to work with any React application.

Preparing the environment

To prepare the environment, we'll take the previous code we developed in *Chapter 6, React with Rematch – The Best Couple – Part II*, as the base application that is going to be tested with testing libraries such as Jest and Testing Library.

To make use of these libraries, first we must install them as `dev` dependencies using Yarn as we did in *Chapter 6, React with Rematch – The Best Couple – Part II*:

```
yarn add --dev jest esbuild-jest msw whatwg-fetch
```

We're installing some interesting dependencies. Let's explain them:

- `jest`: As we explained in the previous section, Jest is the most powerful JavaScript testing framework out there, with an amazing focus on simplicity.

- `esbuild-jest`: Since we're using Vite, which uses `esbuild` under the hood, an extremely fast JavaScript bundler written in Go, the recommended approach is to transform our source code in the Jest tests in the same way that our application will be built. In some cases where Vite isn't used, such as in Babel projects, we can use the `babel-jest` package directly to transform our source code.

- `msw`: As we explained previously, instead of mocking every function that contains a request, we just intercept these requests and mock them on the network level.

- `whatwg-fetch`: Since Jest runs in a Node.js environment where the browser API isn't available, `whatwg-fetch` is a **polyfill** to make it available. To be clear, a polyfill is a piece of code that provides the technology that the developer expects the system to provide natively, but since the `fetch()` interface only works in browser environments, this polyfill makes `fetch()` also works in Node.js environments. This won't translate into an impact on our bundle size, since it's just a dev dependency for our Jest tests.

Now, we can start developing our model's tests, but since we're also going to use the Testing Library tool, let's install all the required packages:

```
yarn add --dev @testing-library/{dom,jest-dom,react,user-event}
```

Like we did for the previous script, let's define the packages:

- `@testing-library/react`: This is the main library package. It's a very lightweight solution for testing React components with functions on top of `react-dom` and `react-dom/test-utils`, in a way that encourages better testing practices.

- `@testing-library/dom`: The DOM Testing Library package helps us in testing DOM nodes simulated by JS-DOM provided by Jest or in the browser, and provides a set of utilities for querying the DOM for nodes in a similar way to how the user finds elements on the page; for instance, `getByText("Cart")` will search for a DOM element where the text is `Cart`.

- `@testing-library/jest-dom`: This library provides a set of custom Jest matchers that you can use to extend Jest with Testing Library methods.

- `@testing-library/user-event`: This library tries to simulate real events that would happen in the browser as the user interacts with it. For example, `userEvent.click(checkbox)` would change the state of the checkbox.

> **Important note**
>
> If some definitions are unclear or you need to extend these definitions, feel free to check the official website of Testing Library (`https://testing-library.com`), which is great and will help you to understand this chapter even more. In any case, I'll explain with examples in the *Creating tests for React components* section of this chapter, where we'll learn when to use this code, how it works, and how it tests our components.

Jest needs some initial configuration to make it work, so we need to create a `jest.config.js` file to configure Jest a bit for our needs, transforming our source code to make it interpretable by Jest and setting up MSW.

Configuring Jest

First, create a `jest.config.js` file in root of your website that contains the following:

```
module.exports = {
  transform: {
    "^.\\.jsx?$": "esbuild-jest"
  },
  setupFilesAfterEnv: ["./test/setup-env.js"]
}
```

This exports a simple configuration of Jest that will transform all the .js and .jsx files using the esbuild-jest transformer. setupFilesAfterEnv allows us to define a list of paths to modules that will run some code to set up our testing suite properly. This code will run before each test, so this is extremely useful for configuring our MSW mocks.

Now, we can add some additional scripts to package.json to run the Jest framework when we end up configuring these frameworks:

```json
"scripts": {
    "test": "jest",
    "test:watch": "jest --watch",
    "test:coverage": "jest --coverage",
    "lint": "eslint src --ext .js,.jsx",
    "start:api": "json-server --watch api/db.json --port 8000",
    "dev": "concurrently 'yarn start:api' 'vite'",
    "build": "vite build",
    "serve": "concurrently 'yarn start:api' 'vite preview'"
},
```

We modified our package.json file to include three new scripts:

- yarn test: for running Jest as a single run, will run the whole testing suite just once.

- yarn test:watch: will run in watch mode; this mean that Jest framework will open a tool inside your terminal and will auto run the tests you introduce or change.

- yarn test:coverage: to check that our application is correctly covered, Jest offers a **Command-Line Interface (CLI)** argument called --coverage to analyze and compare whether there's something that we didn't test and we should. A safe coverage value should be between 70 and 80%, though we'll try to get 100% in this chapter.

Configuring MSW

To configure MSW, we need to create three files: setup-env.js, server.js, and server-handlers.js.

Let's start with the first one that is required by the previous jest.config.js file.

You must create a folder called `test/` in the root folder, and inside this folder create the `setup-env.js` file. The `setup-env.js` file will contain all the code we want to run before each test:

```js
import "whatwg-fetch";
import "@testing-library/jest-dom";

import { server } from "./server";

window.IntersectionObserver = jest.fn(function () {
  this.observe = jest.fn();
  this.disconnect = jest.fn();
});

beforeAll(() => server.listen());
afterEach(() => server.resetHandlers());
afterAll(() => server.close());
```

In this file, we're doing three things: the first one is is importing the `whatwg-fetch` polyfill, which as you'll remember is required to make the `fetch()` API work in Jest, and the second import is importing the `jest-dom` utility function to our Jest framework; we'll see the benefit of this function later.

The second one is importing the `./server` file, which is still not created. We're going to create a server to intercept the requests of our application and mock the results, which is why we use the `beforeAll()`, `afterEach()`, and `afterAll()` methods to listen before any test, to reset the handler after each test, and to close when all the tests end.

And the last one is mocking the `IntersectionObserver` API, like the `fetch()` API, because `IntersectionObserver` isn't available in the browser, so we must mock these methods to be able to run the testing suite correctly.

Now, let's create the `server.js` file:

```js
import { setupServer } from "msw/node";
import { handlers } from "./server-handlers";

const server = setupServer(...handlers);

export { server };
```

`server.js` is the file responsible for importing the main code required to make MSW work. We import `setupServer(...handlers)` to launch the server with the mocked handlers. As you remember, in the `setup-env` file we were running some methods of this exported `server` property, `.listen()`, `.resetHandlers()`, and `.close()`, so remember to export it.

Now, we're ready to intercept the requests that our application is making when entering a page; MSW uses this server to return mocked data for testing purposes. You might think that this type of mocking makes no sense when we're already mocking the data when launching the `json-server` library, but in real-world applications, you won't be mocking the data, so this chapter will be really useful to help you migrate real-world applications.

Of course, feel free to check the documentation of MSW if you have any additional queries about how this mocking system works: `https://mswjs.io`.

Now, let's create the `server-handlers.js` file, probably the most important since it will be responsible for defining the mocked return of our API:

```
import { rest } from "msw";
import { products } from "../api/db.json";


export const handlers = [];
```

We're importing the `rest` handler. This request handler exports some methods such as `.get()`, `.post()`, and `.patch()` as a REST API exposes, so we can easily define the first method we're calling in our application:

```
export const handlers = [
  rest.get("http://localhost:8000/products", (req, res, ctx) =>
{
    const limit = req.url.searchParams.get("_limit");
    const header = { "x-total-count": products.length };
    return res(ctx.set(header), ctx.json(products.slice(0,
    limit)));
  }),
```

We're adding to the `handlers` array a new request handler for the `.get()` method and providing a request path, in our case, `http://localhost:8000/products` because our application will use this URL to recover the products. We define the domain to be able to intercept the requests as they come, like a real API. Then, this function has a response resolver, which means that we're returning a header with `products.length` and the products sliced to the limit passed to this request. Now, we're able to test any part of our code that calls asynchronously to this resource.

But, as you'll remember, we also implemented a `.patch()` method in our application to add products to the favorites or remove them, so let's mock that too:

```
rest.patch("http://localhost:8000/products/:id", (req, res,
ctx) => {
    const { favorite } = req.body;
    const { id } = req.params;
    const modifiedProduct = products.find((p) => p.id === id);
    modifiedProduct.favorite = favorite;
    return res(ctx.json(modifiedProduct));
  }),
];
```

We just need to add a new method following another request method, inside the `handlers` array, but in this case with `rest.patch()`. This request path contains a dynamic `:id` parameter, which will be used later to find that product in the JSON and modify it to finally return the modified product to the request with the `res` parameter.

Now we have all our application requests mocked and ready to be tested. Also, we configured all the minimal configuration that Jest and Testing Library need, so let's move on to start writing our first test.

In the next section, we'll see how to test Rematch models and how easy it is to dispatch and test business logic that's encapsulated inside Rematch models.

Creating tests for Rematch models

> **Tip**
>
> Before getting started with this section, I recommend taking a first look at the Jest documentation, `https://jestjs.io`, and discovering which assertions are available to understand this chapter even more. Along the chapter we'll explain in detail what they do and how Jest simplifies the testing process.

To get started, take a look at this code, which will be the pattern that we'll reuse for our tests:

```
describe("Describe the suite", () => {
   beforeEach(() => {})
   beforeAll(() => {})
   afterEach(() => {})
   afterAll(() => {})

   it("should do ...", () => {
      expect(1).toEqual(1)
   })
})
```

In all the tests that we are going to create, we'll define the `describe()` method, which allows us to gather our tests into separate groupings within the same file. In this way, we can describe the component name and just write in the `it()` method what the component should do.

Also, Jest exposes some helper functions to handle situations where our tests need to do or execute some code before tests run, or after they end. In our case, we'll use `beforeEach()` to reset the Rematch store to its initial state, so every `it()` test will contain a restored state of every model so subsequent tests will be independently of each other.

Now we can use one of two ways of organizing our testing files structure:

- Create a folder that contains all the tests.
- Create them together with the source code file.

We'll pick the last one, both for simplicity purposes and also for discovering quickly which parts of our code are being untested.

So, let's start by creating a `cart.test.js` file inside `/src/store/models/`. We'll have the `cart.js` source code and `cart.test.js` together.

We can start by testing whether the initial state of our cart is correctly returned and contains what we expect it to contain:

```
import { store, dispatch } from "../index";
const getCart = () => store.getState().cart;

describe("Cart model", () => {
```

```
it("should return the initial state correctly", () => {
    expect(getCart()).toEqual({ addedIds: [], quantityById: {}
    });
});
});
```

As we'll use the `store.getState().cart` method a lot in our tests, we can write little functions to make it a bit easier to access these values. We can do this so our test is expecting that our cart state will be equal to a property called `addedIds` with an empty array and a `quantityById` property with an empty object.

We can test whether this code works by just running the following in our terminal:

```
yarn test
```

We'll see that our terminal will log something like this:

```
$ jest
 PASS  src/store/models/cart.test.js
  Cart model
   ✓ should return the initial state correctly (2 ms)
 Tests:       1 passed, 1 total
```

We already have our first model test and it's correctly passing because our state returns these values correctly.

Now, we can test a critical situation. Imagine some developer introduces some extra logic to the `ADD_TO_CART` reducer and breaks the current implementation of adding a product to the cart. We would lose sales and revenue by not having this tested, so let's test it:

```
it("should ADD_TO_CART", () => {
    dispatch.cart.ADD_TO_CART({ id: "ID" });
    expect(getCart()).toEqual({
        addedIds: ["ID"],
        quantityById: {
            ID: 1,
        },
    }),
});
```

We're dispatching the `ADD_TO_CART` reducer of the store that was previously imported; we expect that when this reducer is dispatched, the cart will contain the corresponding ID and the correct quantity:

```
PASS  src/store/models/cart.test.js
  Cart model
    ✓ should return the initial state correctly (2 ms)
    ✓ should ADD_TO_CART
Tests:       2 passed, 2 total
```

Our tests passed and we're sure that this logic won't be broken by any change. But there's a lot of logic yet to test, so let's test the scenario where we add the same product twice. As you'll remember, this reducer modifies the `quantityById` object, increasing the current value, but doesn't add the same ID to the `addedIds` array because it is already in the array, so let's do this:

```
it("should increase an already added item to the cart", () => {
    dispatch.cart.ADD_TO_CART({ id: "ID" });
    dispatch.cart.ADD_TO_CART({ id: "ID" });
    expect(getCart()).toEqual({
      addedIds: ["ID"],
      quantityById: {
        ID: 2,
      },
    });
});
```

Will this test pass? I can tell you that this test is not going to pass… because we're not resetting the state of our model, `beforeEach()`. So, if we run our test suite, we'll see that this test is failing because instead of `quantityById` being 2, it will be 3 because the previous `it()` function already added the same product ID.

It's safer to reset the previous state on each `it()` function. Also, you could create a brand-new store before every test, rather than having one store and resetting it. Since we haven't tried `rootReducers` yet, we're going with the first approach.

In this way, we achieve encapsulated `it()` functions with their own testing logic and state, which are easy to predict and debug. To do this, we just need to use `rootReducers`, but what is `rootReducers`? Sometimes, we don't need an entire model to create a Redux reducer, so Rematch allows us to introduce a new section in the `init()` method with `rootReducers`. This `rootReducers` object can be called from anywhere and works as it works in Redux.

So, now our store `init()` method will look like this:

```
export const store = init({
  models: { shop, cart },
  redux: {
    rootReducers: {
      RESET: () => undefined,
    },
  },
});
```

We created a root reducer called `RESET` that returns `undefined`. When a root reducer returns `undefined`, it resets every Rematch model to its initial state.

Now, in `cart.test.js`, we can add a `beforeEach()` line to reset the state before each `it()` test:

```
describe("Cart model", () => {
  beforeEach(() => dispatch({ type: "RESET" }));
```

If we run `yarn test` again, we'll see that our testing suite is passing correctly.

To avoid making this chapter longer, I encourage you to introduce the tests I've given here and compare them with the implementation in the code provided in the official *Redux Made Easy with Rematch* repository on GitHub:

- Decrease an already added product of the cart.
- Remove completely a product from the cart.
- Reset the cart to its initial state via an internal reducer.

If you're able to create all of these tests, you'll have the cart model with 100% coverage and be one step closer to our main objective, getting a complete application fully tested.

Now, we can move on to the next model test, the shop model, where we'll test asynchronous code and run effects inside tests. As you'll remember, we implemented an interceptor to be able to test this test since it uses the `fetch()` interface to recover products from the API.

In this test, we're going to make sure that the `getProducts()` effect returns the expected products correctly, and we'll test that adding a product to the favorites dispatches the effect and correctly returns the product with the `favorite` attribute changed.

Let's start by creating a new file called `shop.test.js` inside `/src/store/models`. Remember to define the `beforeEach` method to reset the store on every `it()` function.

As Rematch is compatible with `async/await` keywords, and Jest is also compatible, we can directly use an `async` keyword in our `it()` function and await our effect to be dispatched:

```
it("should run getProducts and recover 10 products", async ()
=> {
  await dispatch.shop.getProducts();
  expect(getShop().products).toHaveLength(10);
  expect(getShop().totalCount).toEqual(1000);
});
```

It seems incredible that these two lines of code fully test that our effect is calling to our API, which is intercepted by MSW, which returns the `db.json` products and then passes to the reducer and adds the returned products to the desired state, but yes, it's doing that.

This test was easy, but what about adding a product to favorites and checking that it's correctly added?

```
it("should run setFavorite affect and modify the favorite
property", async () => {
  await dispatch.shop.getProducts();
  const productToFind = getShop().products[0];
  expect(productToFind.favorite).toEqual(true);
  await dispatch.shop.setToFavorite({
    id: productToFind.id,
  });
  expect(getShop().products[0].favorite).toEqual(false);
});
```

As we reset our state on every test, the first step of our test after the cleanup is to run the get Products effect again to return the first 10 products. After that, we take the first product of our list and we assign it to a variable called productToFind. In this case, we expect that this product was already a favorite in our list, so we expect that after running the setToFavorite effect, our state should contain the same product but with favorite set to true or false given the original value; we're just toggling the initial value to be the opposite.

As you can see, testing asynchronous code with Rematch is as simple as using an async/await keyword. The business logic is clear and maintainable.

There's a pending test that I recommend doing to achieve 100% coverage of this test, which is testing the filterByName() utility function we use in the get Products effect when the user searches in the header. It expects root State as the first parameter and the second parameter is the product name to search. Give it a try; if you get stuck, feel free to check the official code in the GitHub repository.

If we run the yarn test:coverage command, we'll see that our models are near to being totally covered. Anyway, a value between 70 and 80% is already high, so 95.65% is incredible because sometimes it's impossible to test 100% of the code:

src/store/models		95.65	66.67	100	100
cart.js		95.45	75	100	100
shop.js		95.83	50	100	100

In the next section, we'll push forward to improve our testing suite even more, and we're going to use a Testing Library package to test our React components as the user will see them in the browser. These tests will give us the confidence to refactor the user interface and be sure that the functionality of the application isn't broken.

Creating tests for React components

As developers, we don't want complex development experiences where we get slowed down or, even worse, the entire team gets slowed down by complex architectures and libraries that make software unmaintainable. The React Testing Library is a lightweight solution for testing React components. It provides utility functions on top of react-dom to query the DOM in the same way the user would.

Understanding this as we did in the previous section, I'm going to explain the principal methods we're going to use, but I encourage you to have a read of the Testing Library website:

```
import { render, screen } from "@testing-library/react"

describe("described suite", () => {
  it("should render correctly", () => {
    render(<SomeComponent />)
    expect(screen.queryByText("some text in the screen")).
    toBeInTheDocument()
  })
})
```

One of the benefits of using Jest is that Testing Library doesn't work on its own because it needs a test runner, so Jest, together with JS-DOM, a pure JavaScript implementation of many web standards, is able to emulate a subset of the browser features in Node.js environments well enough.

We can use `describe()` and `it()` in the same way that we did in the previous tests, but now, instead of testing the store, we use a utility function called `render()` exported by the Testing Library package. It's self-explanatory since this function will create a `div` element and append that `div` element to `document.body`, and there, the component we pass to this function will be rendered, as we do in real React applications.

Also, you'll check that we're using the `screen.` object, which has every query that is pre-bound to `document.body`, so you can use any Testing Library query to the previously rendered component.

Queries are the methods that Testing Library exports to find elements on the page. Depending on what page content you're selecting, different queries may be more or less appropriate, so feel free to check the official Testing Library documentation about queries to make use of the most accessible ones.

To get started with the easier ones, let's start with the `Header` component and check that it is rendered correctly with the values we expect to see.

Create a file inside `src/components` called `Header.test.jsx`:

```
describe("Header", () => {
  it("should be rendered correctly", () => {
    render(<Header />);
    expect(screen.queryByText("Ama")).toBeInTheDocument();
    expect(screen.queryByText("zhop")).toBeInTheDocument();
    expect(screen.queryByRole("textbox")).toBeInTheDocument();
    expect(screen.queryByRole("button")).toBeInTheDocument();
  });
```

We're checking with these assertions that our logo is split into two elements, which is why we use two `queryByText` functions, then we test whether one textbox is a renderer and that the **RESET** button of our textbox is also rendered.

Now, we can test that writing some text inside our textbox correctly changes the value of the textbox. This is a good test since our component is a controlled one, so this behavior could fail easily to add new features to this component:

```
  it("should change the input text value", () => {
    render(<Header />);
    const input = screen.getByRole("textbox");
    userEvent.type(input, "Some search value");
    expect(input).toHaveValue("Some search value");
  });
```

We're rendering the `Header` component again, then after that, we get the textbox and use it to type as the user does, and we expect that the value of the input will be equal to the typed text of the user. To be able to test these scenarios where we need to test an user interaction, we must install and import `@testing-library/user-event`.

`userEvent` is the import of the following:

```
import userEvent from "@testing-library/user-event";
```

Testing Library offers a lot of official and unofficial solutions to handle complex situations such as clicks, double-clicks, keyboard commands, tab keypresses, and even hover and unhover actions. The `user-event` library exports a lot of utility methods to make these things easier.

As we did in the previous section, give it a go and try to implement a new test that resets the input text value once something is already written, querying the **RESET** button and clicking it. After that, the input value should be empty. Feel free to check the solution proposed in the code located in the GitHub repository.

What about creating a test that needs or uses Redux hooks, such as `useDispatch` or `useSelector`?

We could wrap our component with the `Provider` component that `react-redux` exposes on every `render()` method of our tests, like this:

```
render(<Provider store={store}><Header /></Provider>);
```

It will work, yes, but is it readable? No. Since Testing Library is super customizable, it allows us to extend the `render` functionality by creating utility functions with shared logic to reuse those functions in our tests. That's why we're going to create a new function called `renderWithRematchStore(view, store)`.

In this function, instead of passing the current store instance, we could create a brand-new store and return it to the test function; this way, every test will have its own store instead of sharing the same instance and resetting the state So, create a file inside `src/test/` called `utils.jsx`:

```jsx
import React from "react";
import { render } from "@testing-library/react";
import { Provider } from "react-redux";
export const renderWithRematchStore = (ui, store) =>
  render(ui, {
    wrapper: ({ children }) => (
      <Provider store={store}>
        {children}
      </Provider>
    ),
  });
```

We're taking any component as a first parameter and any store as a second parameter, and the `render()` method accepts as an option a wrapper property, which is a React component. In our case, we render the `Provider` component provided by `react-redux`.

Now, for example, we could test what happens when the user writes in the input and presses the *Enter* key – it should change a value in our store, right?

```
it("should dispatch an action to the store when pressing
Enter", () => {
    renderWithRematchStore(<Header />, store);
    const input = screen.getByRole("textbox");
    userEvent.type(input, "Some search value");
    expect(input).toHaveValue("Some search value");
    userEvent.keyboard("[Enter]");
    expect(store.getState().shop.query).toEqual("Some search
    value");
});
```

We use the `userEvent` library to type and to handle the *Enter* keypress, and after that, we check that our store correctly contains the text that the user has written in the input.

There are a lot of tests that can be written using the Testing Library superpowers, which is why we're going to introduce the first ones to every component of our application, and you are free to introduce the suggested ones.

Inside `src/components/Cart`, we have two components, the `Cart` component itself and `CartProduct`, so let's start with the `Cart` component. We want to check that it's initially rendered correctly:

```
describe("Cart", () => {
    beforeEach(() => dispatch({ type: "RESET" }));
    it("should render the cart component", () => {
        renderWithRematchStore(<Cart />, store);
        expect(screen.queryByText("Clear")).toBeInTheDocument();
        expect(screen.queryByText("Your total cart:")).
        toBeInTheDocument();
        expect(screen.queryByText("$0.00")).toBeInTheDocument();
    });
```

We're expecting that our `Cart` component, connected to the Rematch store, correctly renders a button with the text **Clear**, and also that it contains the **Your total cart: $0.00** label. Incredibly, we're already testing whether the function that formats our numbers is working correctly.

In this component, I also tested the following:

- Renders a product on the cart and the total price is re-calculated
- Renders two products and the price is re-calculated
- Should reset the cart to its initial state when clicking the **Clear** button
- Should increase the quantity of the products in the cart, using the + button
- Should decrease the quantity of the products in the cart, using the – button
- Should remove a product from the cart completely

With these tests added to `Cart.test.jsx`, we got 100% coverage of our `Cart` component, so let's move on to test `CartProduct`.

Create a file inside `src/components/Cart`, called `CartProduct.test.jsx`:

```
describe("CartProduct", () => {
  it("should render the quantity correctly", () => {
    const { container } = render(
      <CartProduct product={productJson} quantity={1423} />
    );
    expect(screen.queryByLabelText("product quantity")).
    toContainHTML("1423");
    expect(container).toMatchSnapshot();
  });
});
```

In this test, we're just checking that passing a custom quantity correctly renders the custom quantity, and then we expect that the container element matches the snapshot.

With these tests completely introduced, we have 100% coverage of our `Cart` system:

```
src/components/Cart         |      100 |      100 |      100 |
100 |
  Cart.jsx                  |      100 |      100 |      100 |
100 |
  CartProduct.jsx           |      100 |      100 |      100 |
100 |
```

Now, we can test `ProductList`, which contains the `List` and `Product` components. Let's start by creating two new files, `List.test.jsx` and `Product.test.jsx`.

Let's start with `List`, which renders a list and 10 list items in the first render:

```
describe("List", () => {
  beforeEach(() => dispatch({ type: "RESET" }));
  it("should render the first ten products correctly", async ()
  => {
    renderWithRematchStore(<List />, store);
    expect(await screen.findByRole("list", { name: "" })).
    toBeInTheDocument();
    expect((await screen.findAllByRole("listitem")).length).
    toEqual(10);
  });
});
```

We're using the `async/await` keyword because you'll remember that the `getProducts()` effect is a promise that will be resolved once our API returns the data coming from the backend, so we await the promise of the `findByRole` method to be resolved, which will mean that this method correctly waited and found the given element. The promise will be rejected if no element is found after a timeout of 1 second.

Now, to test the `Product` component, we can create a suite where we mix a mocked prop product and the product connected to a Rematch store. Initially, we could just check that the `Product` component is rendered correctly:

```
describe("Product", () => {
  it("should render the product correctly", () => {
    render(<Product product={productJson} />);


    expect(screen.queryByText(productJson.productName)).
    toBeInTheDocument();
```

```
  expect(
    screen.queryByText(productJson.productDescription)
  ).toBeInTheDocument();
  expect(screen.queryByRole("img")).toBeInTheDocument();
  expect(screen.queryByText("$1.00")).toBeInTheDocument();
  expect(screen.queryByText("No stock")).toBeInTheDocument();
  expect(screen.queryByText("Add to cart")).
  toBeInTheDocument();
  expect(screen.queryByText("Add to cart")).toBeDisabled();
});
```

We expect that our screen is correctly rendering all the elements we expect our product to contain: the title, the image, the price, the button for adding to cart, and the stock indicator.

Now, as we have the `productJson` variable, which is just an object with one product schema (you can use one of the `db.json` files), we can spread this variable to fit our needs. For example, say we want to test what happens when the product has stock:

```
it("should render stock if the product has stock", () => {
  render(<Product product={{ ...productJson, stock: 1 }} />);
  expect(screen.queryByText("In stock")).toBeInTheDocument();
  expect(screen.queryByText("Add to cart")).toBeEnabled();
});
```

We spread the `productJson` variable and we modify the stock to 1, then we expect that our product must render **In stock** and the **Add to cart** button must be enabled.

In the same way, we can use it to test what happens when the product is a favorite or not:

```
it("should paint the favorite button red, when favorite is on",
() => {
  render(<Product product={{ ...productJson, favorite: true
  }} />);
  expect(screen.queryByLabelText("like")).
  toBeInTheDocument();
  expect(screen.queryByLabelText("like")).toHaveClass("text-
  red-500");
});
```

```
it("should NOT paint the favorite button, when favorite is
off", () => {
    render(<Product product={productJson} />);
    expect(screen.queryByLabelText("like")).
    toBeInTheDocument();
    expect(screen.queryByLabelText("like")).toHaveClass("text-
    gray-400");
});
```

Here, we have two tests where we test what class has the favorite element. If it is a favorite, it must contain the text-red-500 class, which makes the heart icon red, and when it's in its default state, it must be just text-gray-400.

Testing class names as we did in the previous test is usually a bad idea since they tend to change and are not a good indicator of things going well. It's encouraged to add accessibility labels like aria-label that describe the current icon's meaning, basically you describe what behavior is occurring in that moment, and instead of doing the test against a class, you do the test against that label.

React Testing Library makes these kind of tests as easy as using screen.getByLabelText(), where you must pass the aria-label you used to describe the element as first argument.

As we did in other situations, now we can also introduce tests with the Rematch store for this component since it uses the dispatch method internally that Rematch exposes.

We can now test that our Product component correctly dispatches the ADD_TO_CART reducer and correctly changes the Cart state:

```
it("should dispatch add to cart when has stock", () => {
    renderWithRematchStore(<Product product={{
    ...productJson, stock: 1 }} />, store );
    expect(screen.queryByText("Add to cart")).
    toBeInTheDocument();
    userEvent.click(screen.queryByText("Add to cart"));
    expect(store.getState().cart).toEqual({
        addedIds: ["b590e450-1e0c-4344-92b8-e1f6cc260587"],
        quantityById: {
            "b590e450-1e0c-4344-92b8-e1f6cc260587": 1,
        },
    });
```

In this test, we're querying the **Add to cart** button and clicking it, and then we expect that our cart model state will be changed to the correct ID and quantity. In this way, we're correctly testing that any product of our store can flow through the entire business logic. Pressing the button correctly dispatches the reducer, which correctly modifies the state, from React to Rematch.

I also recommend testing some extra behaviors such as the following:

- Should not dispatch when the product doesn't have stock

- Should change the favorite button when clicking on it and execute the `dispatch` method

With all these tests introduced, we can check whether we're near 100% coverage with these tests:

src/components/ProductList	97.06	90.91	92.31	96.55
List.jsx	95.24	80	87.5	94.44
Product.jsx	100	100	100	100
index.jsx	100	100	100	100

But what about the total coverage? Run `yarn test:coverage` on your terminal and check that correctly our testing suite is displaying a 98.8% level of coverage:

File	% Stmts	% Branch	% Funcs	% Lines
All files	98.8	82.76	98.51	99.29

We achieved an amazing 98.8%, but what's pending on our side to achieve 100% coverage? After running `yarn test:coverage`, a folder called `coverage/` will be created in the root of your project, and inside will be an `lcov-report/` folder that contains a static website for analyzing which lines aren't covered or need additional care:

All files

98.79% Statements 163/165   **85.19%** Branches 23/27   **98.48%** Functions 65/66   **99.28%** Lines 138/139

Press *n* or */* to go to the next uncovered block, *b*, *p* or *k* for the previous block.

File ▲		Statements		Branches		Functions		Lines	
src/components		100%	11/11	75%	3/4	100%	5/5	100%	10/10
src/components/Cart		100%	30/30	100%	2/2	100%	14/14	100%	25/25
src/components/ProductList		97.06%	33/34	90.91%	10/11	92.31%	12/13	96.55%	28/29
src/store		100%	6/6	100%	0/0	100%	2/2	100%	5/5
src/store/models		98%	49/50	80%	8/10	100%	18/18	100%	43/43
src/utils		100%	10/10	100%	0/0	100%	6/6	100%	7/7
test		100%	24/24	100%	0/0	100%	8/8	100%	20/20

Figure 7.1 – lcov-report website of this chapter's testing suite

In our case, we can check the `src/components/ProductList/List` component. Line 20 isn't covered since we're not testing the infinite scroll implementation, and since we're using a simulation of the browser for testing, this use case should probably be tested inside an end-to-end testing suite such as Cypress that runs our application and our tests inside a real browser environment where the scroll behavior is not simulated but is actually tested by users.

The question is whether we should use unit testing, integration testing, or end-to-end testing. You should use all of them and decide which types of testing fit your requirements and the quirks of your application.

In this section, we discovered how Testing Library makes testing React components much easier than we initially expected and how Rematch and Testing Library can work together to make the testing suite of our application as close to the reality of how our users will use our application as possible, giving us the confidence to add new features or refactor existing ones.

Summary

In this chapter, we have learned how to correctly test a complete application with side effects and complex logic as if it was a real shop with a cart system. Also, we have learned how to handle asynchronous operations to an external API with Rematch, and how this entire logic can be encapsulated inside Rematch models and tested easily for reuse in other applications.

In the next chapter, we'll iterate over this application using all the superpowers that Rematch offers thanks to its official Rematch plugin ecosystem. We'll introduce automatic loading/success behaviors, selectors for memoizing computed values, and even persisting the cart in the browser storage. In summary, we'll analyze how Rematch plugins work internally and the story behind them.

8
The Rematch Plugins Ecosystem

In this chapter, we'll learn how Rematch plugins are built and which hooks are exposed for interacting with our store and models. We'll look at the most common use cases of each hook and how they work internally. Also, we'll focus on the official list of plugins provided by Rematch, analyzing their internal architecture and configuring them inside our Amazhop application.

In this chapter, we'll cover the following topics:

- Introduction to Rematch plugins
- The Rematch loading plugin
- The Rematch select plugin
- The Rematch Immer plugin
- The Rematch updated plugin
- The Rematch persist plugin

By the end of the chapter, you will understand how Rematch plugins extend the functionality of Rematch with minimal impact on your bundle size and performance, even improving performance in some cases. Also, you will learn how they work internally and how they can be used in a real application.

Technical requirements

To follow along with this chapter, you will need the following:

- Basic knowledge of **Vanilla JavaScript** and **ES6** features
- Basic knowledge of **HTML5** features
- **Node.js >= 12**
- Basic knowledge of **React** and **CSS**
- A browser (**Chrome** or **Firefox**, for instance)
- A code editor (**Visual Studio Code**, for instance)

You can find the code for this chapter in the book's GitHub repository: `https://github.com/PacktPublishing/Redux-Made-Easy-with-Rematch/tree/main/packages/chapter-8`.

To get started with this chapter, we'll use the application we implemented in *Chapter 6, React with Rematch - The Best Couple - Part II*, as a template to add our Rematch plugins. This chapter will give you an understanding of how Rematch plugins work and how to add them to any Rematch application.

Introduction to Rematch plugins

Probably the first question that we should ask is *what is a plugin?* A plugin is a software add-on that is installed on software, enhancing its capabilities. When we think about how plugins work, what comes to our minds are browser extensions where the browser has just minimal functionality, or, better put, just what's needed for most users.

Making software extendable using plugins is a breeze because our base software is simple and plugins can extend this base functionality, making the software even more powerful but covering all use cases. If a user only wants the base software, they can decide to not use plugins, and if another user has a complex use case, they can implement a plugin that covers that use case without jamming other users. Sometimes building moldable software is the best approach.

Rematch is one of the best examples of modularity, and offering plugins was one of the best decisions we took when building Rematch.

The `@rematch/core` package contains minimal code to make Rematch work with Redux, letting any developer introduce an easy state-management solution to their application with best practices in less than 2 KB.

Rematch plugins provide the ability to extend Rematch functionality by overwriting the configuration, adding new models, or even replacing the whole store with new properties. Every plugin can contain two static properties called `exposed` and `config`, and four hooks. These hooks are executed from the core package and let us enhance the current store.

To understand from a low-level perspective how Rematch plugins are built and which properties are exposed, we can analyze this diagram:

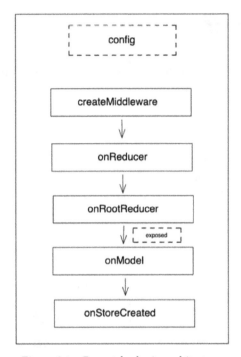

Figure 8.1 – Rematch plugin architecture

Every Rematch plugin can contain any of these properties, so let's explain them.

config

The `config` property is just a plain object with two properties, `models` and `redux`. They allow you to add additional models to the current store. When the store initializes, it will check whether any plugin contains a config schema and will merge our current `init()` configuration with any config from the plugins.

The shape of these properties is the same as the one accepted by the `init()` method. In the next section, *The Rematch loading plugin*, we'll see how these properties let us configure an extra model to handle the loading status of our asynchronous effects.

Here's an example of a custom config inside a plugin:

```
const plugin = {
    config: {
        redux: {
            combineReducers: customCombineReducers,
        }
    },
}
```

In this source code, we're adding a custom `combineReducers` function via the plugin, but we could change any value of the `redux` configuration.

exposed

The `exposed` property allows you to assign extra properties to the store for communicating between plugins. It's executed before the `onModel` and `onStoreCreated` hooks, allowing us to define custom methods of our plugin that could be called later through the store.

This property can return a plain object or a function that returns an object with custom accessors. If using a function, the Rematch store is passed through the first parameter. This is really useful if you need to recover a value from the current state.

This property is heavily used in the Rematch select plugin. We'll analyze it later, but to understand this concept a bit more, imagine that we want a `debug` method in our store that returns the store state and debugs it inside the browser console:

```
const plugin = {
  exposed: (rematchStore) => ({
    debug: () => console.debug(rematchStore.getState())
  }),
},
```

This plugin will add a property to the store that can be called later with `store.debug()` and will use `console.debug` on the current state.

createMiddleware

The `createMiddleware` property is used for creating a custom middleware that needs access to Rematch internals that are available in the Rematch bag, in the first parameter of this property.

For example, we could create a plugin whose main function is logging the current dispatched action and the next state result:

```
const plugin = {
  createMiddleware: (rematchBag) => (store) => (next) =>
  (action) => {
    console.log('dispatching', action)
    const result = next(action)
    console.log('next state', store.getState())
    return result
  }
}
```

The main difference between Rematch `createMiddleware` and the original implementation of Redux middlewares is that Rematch `createMiddleware` is written as a series of four nested functions since a native Redux middleware is a series of three nested functions. These nested functions let us access the following:

- `rematchBag`: Contains all the properties that Rematch accumulates in the initialization step, including models, Redux configuration, and so on.

- `store`: Contains the two principal functions of Redux, `getState()` and `dispatch()`.

- `next`: Responsible for moving to the next middleware in the chain. If the middleware that is executed next is the last one, it executes the original `store.dispatch` function. Just think about it as the name indicates – executing this function passes to the next middleware in the pipeline.

- `action`: This argument contains the action that is passed through the `dispatch` method.

If you don't need to use the `rematchBag` argument, you can just use the `config.redux.middlewares` property from the `init()` function; there's no need to create a plugin.

onReducer

The `onReducer` hook is executed when a base reducer is created for a model. The main objective of this lifecycle is overwriting the original reducer created by our models, returning a new instance of a new reducer will be enough to get an enhanced reducer.

The use case for this hook is to apply additional libraries to reducers; for instance, Rematch persist uses this hook to persist reducers in a persisted storage, for example, local storage:

```
onReducer(reducer, modelName) {
  const reducerConfig = nestedPersistConfig[modelName]
  if (reducerConfig) {
    return persistReducer(reducerConfig, reducer)
  }
  return undefined
},
```

The onReducer hook passes as the first argument the original reducer reference, the current modelName property – normally it's a string – as the second argument, and the Rematch bag as the third argument.

onRootReducer

The onRootReducer hook acts in the same way as the onReducer hook, but in this case, when a rootReducer object is created in the store, it can return a new rootReducer object, which will overwrite the one created by Rematch.

Let's take the Rematch persist example:

```
onRootReducer(rootReducer) {
  return persistReducer(persistConfig, rootReducer)
},
```

It can also persist in any storage that the rootReducer property defined in the init() method.

onModel

When all the setup for the models is completed, the reducers and dispatchers are created and the onModel hook is executed for each model. Normally, it is used for collecting information about models, reducers, and effects; every time our store adds a new model, this hook is executed. Also, it's useful to overwrite any model for a custom one or create new properties inside an existing model

This hook is also executed every time a model is added dynamically to the store using the `store.addModel()` function. This function allows us to dynamically inject models into our store at any moment; this is a really interesting feature since our store could just contain the minimum models, to initialize faster, and we could then inject models dynamically when they're requested.

This hook is heavily used in the Rematch loading and Rematch updated plugins since they create new models based on other models.

To understand which arguments are returned inside the `onModel` property, we can check this code:

```
const plugin = {
  onModel: (model, rematchBag) => {}
}
```

This code snippet just shows which arguments are passed through the `onModel` hook:

- `model`: This is the actual model reference. When we add a new model to the store using `store.addModel()` or we initialize the store for the first time, `model` notifies every plugin that handles the `onModel` listener of every model that the user passed to the `models` property inside the `init()` function. In this way, we can make changes to any model before the store is created.

- `rematchBag`: Contains all the properties that Rematch accumulates in the initialization step, models, Redux configuration, and so on.

In *Chapter 9, Composable Plugins - Create Your First Plugin*, we'll create a plugin that uses the `onModel` hook and we'll go into more detail on this.

onStoreCreated

`onStoreCreated` is the last hook of any Rematch plugin lifecycle, running at the end when the Rematch store is ready. It can return a new store, in which case, it will overwrite the one created by Rematch.

Usually, `onStoreCreated` is used to add extra properties or functions to the store. For example, the Rematch persist plugin uses `redux-persist` under the hood. We persist the entire store because the `redux-persist` library requires us to do it:

```
onStoreCreated(store) {
  persistor = persistStore(store, persistStoreConfig, callback)
},
```

These are all the lifecycles that Rematch exposes and they can be used to extend Rematch functionality without further problems, making Rematch Core maintainable, smaller, and more modular.

To load any Rematch plugin, we just need to import the desired plugin and add it to the `plugins` array of our `init()` function:

```
import loadingPlugin from '@rematch/loading'
import { init } from '@rematch/core'
import models from './models'

init({
  models,
  plugins: [loadingPlugin()],
})
```

If the plugin itself can be configured, we can pass this configuration through the `loadingPlugin()` initializer.

The Rematch team, in the development process of the library, asked its users which features they were interested in being added as plugins and worked hard to bring them to life. There is a collection of five official plugins, which are going to be explained later in this chapter and put into practice in our Amazhop application.

In the next section, we'll see how Rematch introduced an interesting list of official plugins that are heavily maintained and really recommended to add to any application. We'll start with the Rematch loading plugin, one of the most useful plugins that Rematch offers.

The Rematch loading plugin

The official loading plugin for Rematch adds automated loading indicators for effects. This plugin means that we don't have to worry about managing states such as `loading: true` and `loading: false` by ourselves.

Installing and configuration

To install this plugin, as it is published like the `@rematch/core` package, you can just use yarn:

```
yarn add @rematch/loading
```

This plugin adds just 596 bytes to our application.

The loading plugin accepts one optional argument, which is an object with the following properties:

- `name`: Since this plugin will create a new model for handling all the states of loading our effects, we can overwrite the name of this model. By default, it will be called `loading`.

- `type`: By default, this plugin keeps track of running effects using Booleans, `loading: true` and `loading: false`, but you can change that behavior and use numbers or even detailed statuses, like "error" or "success". If you use `type: "number"`, the plugin will track the number of times an effect was executed, like a counter, and if you use `type: "full"`, each effect will contain an object inside the loading plugin state with this shape:

```
{
    "loading": true,
    "success": false,
    "error": false
}
```

This is super useful for building user interfaces where you should check if the Promise resolved an Error, or to see whether everything went fine.

- `whitelist`: An array of effect names that you want to use the loading plugin for. By default, it's empty because the loading plugin works for all effects.

- `blacklist`: An array of effect names that you don't want to use the loading plugin for – just the opposite of `whitelist`.

This plugin will create a schema based on three groups:

```
{
    "global": true,
    "models:": {
        "count": true
    },
    "effects": {
        "count": {
            "increment": true
        }
    }
}
```

We can use a global state that will be true when any effect in any one of our models is loading. This means that when any of our asynchronous effects in our whole store is not fulfilled, `loading` will be `true`.

This global state is split into three sections:

- `global`: If any effect in our whole store is not fulfilled, this will be `true`.
- `models`: Automatically creates an object with every model of our store, so we can know which models are still loading.
- `effects`: Used to individually track which effect inside a model is still loading.

Basically, the plugin goes from a more general state (`global`) to the most detailed state (`effects`).

Example usage

Taking the application we've been developing in this book, just install the package with `yarn` as mentioned previously and use it directly in our `src/store/index.js` file:

```js
import { init } from "@rematch/core";
import createLoadingPlugin from "@rematch/loading";
import { shop, cart } from "./models";

export const store = init({
  models: { shop, cart },
  redux: {
    rootReducers: {
      RESET: () => undefined,
    },
  },
  plugins: [createLoadingPlugin()],
});
```

After introducing these changes and starting the application with `yarn dev` as usual, you can see that inside our Redux DevTools extension, a new model called `loading` automatically appears that contains the schema previously mentioned:

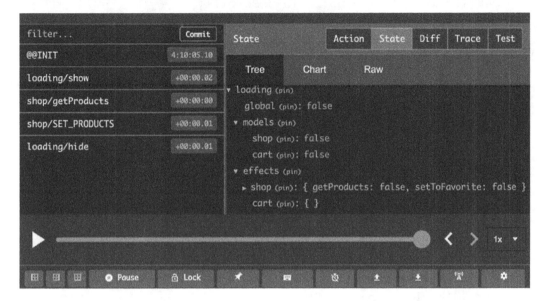

Figure 8.2 – Redux DevTools extension with the @rematch/loading plugin

Imagine a use case where our users enter our shop and they have a poor network connection, such as 3G, meaning our `getProducts()` request takes longer than expected. Right now, a white screen will appear. Let's implement a little spinner that will be shown automatically using the `@rematch/loading` plugin.

To do that, modify our `src/components/List.jsx` component to show a spinner when the `getProducts()` effect is still loading:

```
export const List = () => {
  const isLoading = useSelector(
    (rootState) => rootState.loading.effects.shop.getProducts
  );
```

In this code snippet, we're just using the same strategy we used in other situations to recover data from our store. In this case, we're returning the status of the `getProducts()` effect.

Now, we can modify our infinite scroll hook and tell this hook when our application is still loading and doesn't need to request more data because the previous one is still pending:

```
const [infiniteRef] = useInfiniteScroll({
    loading: isLoading,
```

We can use ternaries in our return function to render a `Spinner` component or return the products list instead. Let's modify our `List` component:

```
<div
    role="list"
    className="grid grid-cols-2 xl:grid-cols-3 2xl:grid-
    cols-4 3xl:grid-cols-5 gap-8 2xl:gap-5 3xl:gap-5"
>
    {products.map((product) => (
        <Product key={product.id} product={product} />
    ))}
</div>
{(isLoading || (hasNextPage && !query)) && (
    <div className="mt-5" ref={infiniteRef}>
        <Spinner />
    </div>
)}
```

We're using the `isLoading` property to indicate when to show the spinner. In our case, we already had this logic, but for the `infiniteRef` reference used to notify `IntersectionObserver` of when to pull more data, we have the OR operand (`||`). This logical operator will return `true` if one of the specified conditions is true. In our case, we'll show the spinner if our application is loading or has more data and the user has scrolled to the bottom.

We can see that when we scroll to the bottom, a spinner appears automatically. Or, if it's the first load, instead of showing just an empty screen, we correctly show the loading indicator:

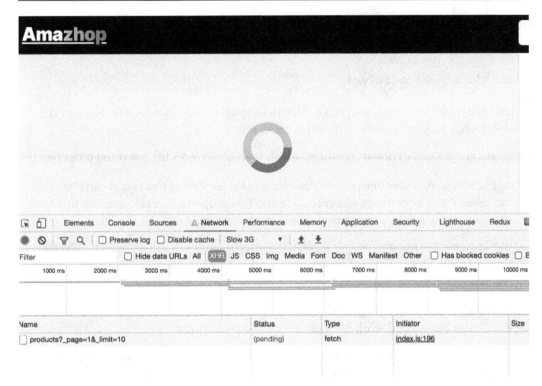

Figure 8.3 – Amazhop showing a loading indicator on first load

In the same way, this feature could be implemented for the favorite button. Since it's an asynchronous effect that uses network resources, it could be delayed due to external factors such as poor connectivity, so it's good to add a spinner for when the user clicks on the favorite button.

In the next section, we'll analyze how the Rematch select plugin works, and how we can improve the performance of our application using selectors.

The Rematch select plugin

Selectors are a really good performance booster for our Rematch/Redux applications. A selector is simply a function that accepts the root state as an argument and returns data that is derived from that root state.

Reselect (`https://github.com/reduxjs/reselect`) is the official library for creating memoized and composable selector functions, and the Rematch select library is built on top of Reselect.

But why are selectors performance boosters? Because selectors aren't recomputed unless one of their arguments changes.

Installing and configuration

To install `@rematch/select`, you can use `yarn` and install it as follows:

```
yarn add @rematch/select
```

This package is just 596 bytes, so it has a minimal impact on our bundle size. None of the official Rematch plugins is more than 600 bytes in size.

This plugin accepts one optional argument, which is an object with the following properties:

- `sliceState`: Sometimes our store is not a plain JavaScript object and can't be accessed using `rootState.model.name`. This property accepts a custom function for getting the model's state based on the store's root state and the model object.
- `selectorCreator`: You can replace the internal Reselect library with a different one by providing a custom function for creating selectors that has the same interface as Reselect.

Usually, the Rematch select plugin won't require any changes in the configuration on your side; the default one should work for most applications out there.

Now, our Rematch model, which has accepted a name, state, reducers, and effects, now also accepts the `selectors` property:

```
selectors: (slice, createSelector) => ({ })
```

The `selectors` property must be a function that accepts the following arguments.

slice

`slice` is the first argument that the `selectors` property returns, and it works in two ways:

- We can create a simple memoized selector based on the current model state:

```
total () {
  return slice(cart =>
    cart.reduce((a, b) => a + (b.price * b.amount), 0)
  )
},
```

This function will only be recomputed when the `cart` state changes.

- `slice` also works as a shortcut to access the current model state. Instead of writing `(rootState) => rootState.currentModel`, we can just use `slice()` and it will return the current state.

createSelector

The `createSelector` function is the default Reselect `createSelector` function. It takes one or more selectors, or an array of selectors, computes their values, and passes them as arguments to the function result.

`createSelector` determines whether the value returned by an input selector has changed between calls using reference equality, `===`. By default, it has a cache size of 1, which means that the selector only stores the preceding value of each input selector.

All these options can be overwritten through the configuration of the plugin using another `selectorCreator` function; for example, Re-reselect, which is built on top of Reselect, tries to enhance selectors with deeper memoization and better cache management:

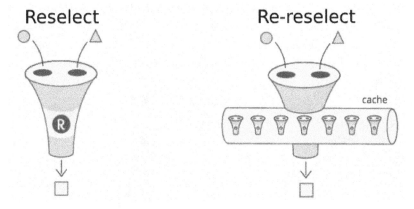

Figure 8.4 – Reselect and Re-reselect comparison

With these concepts clear, we're ready to introduce some selectors in our Amazhop application.

Example usage

Taking the application we've been developing in this book, just install `@rematch/select` with `yarn` and use it directly in our `src/store/index.js` file:

```
export const store = init({
  models: { shop, cart },
  redux: {
```

```
    rootReducers: {
      RESET: () => undefined,
    },
  },
  plugins: [createLoadingPlugin(), createSelectPlugin()],
});
```

Internally, the Rematch select plugin uses the `exposed` property. As you'll remember, this property allows us to expose some extra methods that weren't initially defined.

Looking at our source code, we can easily see that `src/components/Cart/Cart.jsx` needs some selectors, one for recomputing the total price of the cart and one for recovering the products. We start with this:

```
const { addedIds, quantityById } = useSelector((rootState) =>
  rootState.cart);
const cartProducts = useSelector((rootState) =>
  addedIds.map((id) => getProduct(rootState, id))
);
const totalPrice = useSelector((rootState) =>
  addedIds.reduce(
    (total, id) =>
      total + getProduct(rootState, id).price *
      getQuantity(rootState, id),
    0
  )
);
```

But what about if we just implement all this business logic inside our models as selectors and then call them from our React views:

```
const quantityById = useSelector((rootState) => rootState.cart.
quantityById);
const cartProducts = useSelector(store.select.cart.
getCartProducts);
const totalPrice = useSelector(store.select.cart.total);
```

Apart from being cleaner in terms of maintainability, we're extracting logic that could be reused in another view just by using these lines.

Let's go to `src/store/models/cart.js` and introduce a new property called `selectors` that returns `selectors`:

```
selectors: (slice, createSelector) => ({
  total() {
    return createSelector(
      [slice, (rootState) => rootState.shop.products]
      (cartState, products) =>
        cartState.addedIds.reduce(
          (total, id) =>
            total +
              getProduct(products, id).price *
              getQuantity(cartState, id),
          0
        )
    );
  },
})
```

What we did here was just move the logic of the code that we had in `Cart.jsx` to `createSelector`. The first argument of the `createSelector` function is an array with the data used to create the memoized selector, the `slice` function returns the current state, and the second arrow function returns the products of our shop state.

Then, the second argument of the `createSelector` function accesses these values, the first argument, `cartState`, is the `slice` function, and `products` is the arrow function. It is done like this to be able to memoize this selector, meaning that it won't be recomputed unless the `products` array changes.

With this selector introduced, we can use it from the view as we suggested previously:

```
const totalPrice = useSelector(store.select.cart.total);
```

Now, we can implement another selector to return the cart products:

```
getCartProducts() {
  return createSelector(
    [slice, (rootState) => rootState.shop.products],
    (cartState, products) =>
      cartState.addedIds.map((id) => getProduct(products, id))
```

```
    );
  }
```

This selector expects the same data as the `total()` selector, but in this case returns products instead of a number.

Now, thanks to our testing suite, we can run `yarn test` and we can see that our tests passed correctly, meaning that we improved the performance of the application and we're sure that the functionality is still there.

In *Chapter 12, Rematch Performance Improvements and Best Practices*, we'll see how we can optimize these selectors even more, and we'll analyze in depth how to track things and whether our changes correctly reflect a performance boost in our user experience.

One of the most recommended libraries for Redux code bases is **Immer.js**. It's a tiny library of 3 KB that handles immutability with normal JavaScript objects, arrays, and so on, without the requirement of using object spreading, thereby making our code more concise. Rematch offers a plugin that enables Immer by just adding this plugin to our `plugins` property.

The Rematch Immer plugin

As you'll remember from when we spoke about immutability and how Redux and Rematch handle changes of state, Redux forced us to create a new copy of the state on every reducer; we couldn't just mutate the current state and return it because it caused incorrect renders and it's not the correct way of doing things.

Immer.js is a tiny package that allows us to work with immutable state in a more comfortable way because it's based on the copy-on-write mechanism.

The idea is that you will apply your changes to a temporary draft state that is a proxy of the current state. Once all our mutations are done, Immer will produce the next state based on the mutations to the draft state.

To be clearer, instead of spreading and cloning our state all the time, we can just make safe mutations to our state, resulting in an immutable state.

Installation and configuration

To install @rematch/immer, you can use yarn and install it as follows:

```
yarn add @rematch/immer immer
```

`@rematch/immer` has a bundle size of 143 bytes.

Like the other plugins, the Rematch Immer plugin accepts one optional argument, which is an object with the following properties:

- `whitelist`: An array of model names to define which reducers should be wrapped with Immer.

- `blacklist`: An array of model names to define which reducers shouldn't be wrapped with Immer.

  By default, reducers from all models will be wrapped with the `Immer produce` function.

Example usage

Taking the application we've been developing in this book, just install the package with `yarn` and use it directly in our `src/store/index.js` file:

```
export const store = init({
  models: { shop, cart },
  redux: {
    rootReducers: {
      RESET: () => undefined,
    },
  },
  plugins: [
    createLoadingPlugin(),
    createSelectPlugin(),
    createImmerPlugin(),
  ],
});
```

Now, if we run `yarn test`, we'll see some errors related to Immer warnings about not using everything that Immer offers, so let's refactor our model's logic to follow the Immer convention.

Taking the `cart.js` model, we can start refactoring the `ADD_TO_CART` reducer from this:

```
return {
  addedIds: [...state.addedIds, product.id],
  quantityById: {
    ...state.quantityById,
    [product.id]: 1,
  },
};
```

This is the code that `ADD_TO_CART` contains when returning the new state. Now, instead, we can just use mutation functions such as `array.push()`. Do you remember that we couldn't use `.push` because pushing to an array kept the reference? Now, with Immer, we can safely use `.push()` to push to an array:

```
state.addedIds.push(product.id);
state.quantityById[product.id] = 1;
return state;
```

This code snippet of three lines is equivalent to the previous one where we used spread operators and will work as expected. Introducing just a 190-byte plugin makes our code far more readable and maintainable.

Now you can give it a try and refactor the `REMOVE_FROM_CART` reducer where we used the `clonedIds` and `clonedQuantityById` variables, which aren't required with Immer.

Let's now refactor the `SET_FAVORITE` reducer located inside the `shop` model:

```
const products = [...state.products];
products[indexToModify] = product;
return {
  ...state,
  products,
};
```

We refactor it to this one-liner:

```
state.products[indexToModify] = product;
return state;
```

Since we added Immer, it isn't a requirement anymore to clone our arrays or objects to obtain a new reference. This is because Immer resolves this by creating a temporary draft state that is a proxy of the current state; so once we return the state, the mutations are transferred to the next state.

Give it a try and refactor the SET_QUERY and SET_PRODUCTS reducers, and if you get stuck, feel free to check the official *Redux Made Easy with Rematch* GitHub repository. When you think you're done, use yarn test to validate that the suite passes correctly.

The next section is going to be on the Rematch updated plugin, an interesting plugin for situations where we need to track when our promises are dispatched.

The Rematch updated plugin

The Rematch updated plugin is the easiest plugin that we're covering. Basically, it's a plugin for maintaining timestamps when an effect is dispatched.

It can be used to prevent expensive fetch requests within a certain time period or to throttle effects, for example, to avoid users clicking on the same button multiple times within a period of 3 seconds.

Installation and configuration

Install it like all the other official Rematch plugins:

```
yarn add @rematch/updated
```

The updated plugin also accepts some configuration with the following properties:

- name: The name of the model to be created for storing the updated timestamps. By default, it is updated.
- blacklist: An array of model names for which the plugin won't track effects.
- dateCreator: You can pass any custom implementation to create Date objects with custom formatting or a time zone.

We are not going to use the plugin in our application because there's no use case in our application for it.

To conclude this chapter, we will look at the latest official Rematch plugin, the Rematch persist plugin. As the name indicates, this handles persisting our state in different storage services practically out of the box, such as the browser local storage.

The Rematch persist plugin

Last but not least is the Rematch persist plugin, a plugin of just 167 bytes for handling automatic state persistence. It's built on top of the `redux-persist` library (`https://github.com/rt2zz/redux-persist`). We can persist to hundreds of different storage services our whole Rematch store state.

Installation and configuration

Install it like all the other official Rematch plugins:

```
yarn add @rematch/persist redux-persist
```

The Rematch persist plugin also accepts some configuration through four arguments:

- `persistConfig`: This is the first argument and is an object compatible with the `config` argument accepted by the `redux-persist` library.

- `nestedPersistConfig`: Whenever you need to use a nested persist configuration for some models, we can provide an object with a mapping from the model's name to the `redux-persist` config for this model.

- `persistStoreConfig`: The object compatible with the configuration argument accepted by the `redux-persist persistStore` method.

- `callback`: A function called after rehydration is finished. Rehydration means when the `redux-persist` library has already transferred the data saved in the storage to the store.

To introduce this plugin in our application, there are two keys that are always required in our configuration file:

```
import createPersistPlugin from "@rematch/persist"
import localStorage from "redux-persist/lib/storage"


...
plugins: [
  createLoadingPlugin(),
  createSelectPlugin(),
  createImmerPlugin(),
  createPersistPlugin({
    key: "cart-storage",
    storage: localStorage,
```

```
        whitelist: ["cart", "shop"],
    }),
  ],
});
```

The key property is always required since it will be used for defining the key name in the provided storage. Also, the storage allows us to pass custom storage options. In our case, we're going to use the native local storage provided by the browser.

Now, automatically, if we add some products to the cart and reload the page, we'll see that our cart state continues as we had left it before reloading. That's because our Rematch persist plugin persists the whole store inside browser storage after each change in our state. When the store is initialized back, it rehydrates the current state with the persisted one, making changes across our whole state completely persisted to changes on browser or network failures.

We have seen that adding plugins to Rematch is as easy as just installing and adding them to the plugins array of the init() method. They improve the productivity we got initially with Rematch without any inconvenience and make the development experience even better.

Summary

In this chapter, we have learned how Rematch plugins work internally. We've studied in depth which properties and hooks they expose and how those properties are used in real plugins. We have also learned which plugins are official Rematch plugins and how we can use them inside a Rematch application.

In the next chapter, we'll take another step along our learning curve with Rematch: we'll learn how to create a Rematch plugin from the ground up that will be used in our Amazhop application, and how to publish this plugin to NPM to contribute to the open source community.

Section 3: Diving Deeper into Rematch

On completion of this part, you will be able to create your own plugins for your projects. You'll learn how to migrate an existing code base with Rematch and React, written in JavaScript, to TypeScript step by step. You'll also learn how to use Rematch with other frameworks, such as React Native, and how all this code can be optimized using the latest browser, React, and Redux performance optimization techniques.

In this section, we include the following chapters:

- *Chapter 9, Composable Plugins – Create Your First Plugin*
- *Chapter 10, Rewrite a Full Code Base from JavaScript to TypeScript*
- *Chapter 11, Rematch with React Native and Expo – A Real-World Mobile App*
- *Chapter 12, Rematch Performance Improvements and Best Practices*
- *Chapter 13, Conclusion*

9
Composable Plugins – Create Your First Plugin

In this chapter, we'll learn how to create a Rematch plugin that will be used on our Amazhop website, warning us when we dispatch any action with a wrong payload value. Also, we'll learn how we can test this plugin using using Jest, as well as how we can build a module with the latest bundling technologies for publishing it to NPM, making it open source to everyone.

In this chapter, we'll cover the following topics:

- Preparing the environment
- Creating our plugin
- Testing our plugin
- Publishing to NPM

By the end of the chapter, you will understand how to create any Rematch plugin from the ground up with tools for bundling libraries such as Tsdx. You'll also learn how to correctly test these plugins using Jest and how we can use features that Yarn or NPM offer to test these packages locally. Also, you'll learn how to successfully publish a Rematch plugin to NPM.

Technical requirements

To follow along with this chapter, you will need the following:

- Basic knowledge of **Vanilla JavaScript** and **ES6** features

- Basic knowledge of **HTML5** features

- **Node.js >= 12**

- Basic knowledge of **React** and **CSS**

- A browser (**Chrome** or **Firefox**, for instance)

- A code editor (**Visual Studio Code**, for instance)

You can find the code for this chapter in the book's GitHub repository: `https://github.com/PacktPublishing/Redux-Made-Easy-with-Rematch/tree/main/packages/chapter-9`.

To get started with this chapter, we're going to use a different approach to what we did in previous chapters where we built a complete application. In this case, we're going to build a small library that is going to be published to NPM, for further usage in our Amazhop web application.

Preparing the environment

There are multiple ways of creating a library, from using an `index.js` file with one single format and a `package.json` file, to using some JavaScript files that are compiled to multiple formats and published through NPM. We will do the latter.

To compile the JavaScript files, we're going to use a zero-config CLI for package development called **Tsdx** (`https://tsdx.io`). This will help us to develop, test, and publish modern libraries with ease so we can focus on just writing our code and let Tsdx do all the complex configuration.

We can quickly bootstrap a new library in seconds, just by writing this in the terminal:

```
npx tsdx create typed-state-plugin
```

This will create a folder called `typed-state-plugin/` with the basic setup we need to create our library.

This tool is going to create a file structure like this:

```
├── .gitignore
├── .prettierrc
├── package.json
├── src
│   └── index.ts
├── test
│   └── index.test.ts
└── tsconfig.json
```

We won't need anything else, just an `index.ts` file and an `index.test.ts` file for testing our plugin.

The file extension, instead of being `.js` (for JavaScript files), is `.ts` (for TypeScript files). **TypeScript** is an open source language that builds on JavaScript; it basically adds static type definitions, providing us with a way to describe the shape of an object and allowing TypeScript to validate that our code is working as intended.

We can write JavaScript with TypeScript; it's fully compatible. TypeScript is just a higher layer. You can gradually migrate any JavaScript code base to TypeScript since TypeScript compiles any JavaScript files out of the box.

In *Chapter 10, Rewrite a Full Code Base from JavaScript to TypeScript*, we'll analyze in depth how Rematch creates a complete TypeScript system and how the TypeScript language can help us to autocomplete the whole store, giving us the security of knowing what data expects our reducers or effects, or which values are possibly null in our state.

So, what's the current problem we're trying to solve with this plugin?

When we dispatch actions with Redux or Rematch with JavaScript, the `dispatch` method accepts any data as a payload, so we could dispatch data that could break our model's state.

For instance, imagine a scenario where we dispatch an action as follows:

```
dispatch.shop.SET_PRODUCTS({
  products: {}
})
```

This action will dispatch to our reducer a payload with `products` as an object, but if you remember from the code we implemented in the previous chapters, `products` should be an array of objects, not just an object.

JavaScript isn't going to warn us about this and will just fail when, for instance, we try to access at runtime the `products` property as an array:

```
products.forEach(product => products)
```

This will make our application crash because `products` is an object and isn't iterable:

```
VM185:1 Uncaught TypeError: products.forEach is not a function
    at <anonymous>:1:10
```

TypeScript with Rematch brings us the ability to know before the `dispatch` method executes that this code is going to fail, but since our project is still in plain JavaScript, we can build a plugin for checking this at development runtime, warning us if we pass some wrong data to our state.

Basically, we'll shape the schema of our model on each model and when we dispatch any action, this plugin will check whether the payload passed is the one expected by the model's state.

To get started with the code, we need to set up a few `peerDependencies` properties and `devDependencies` properties in our `package.json` file:

```
"peerDependencies": {
    "@rematch/core": "^2",
    "prop-types": "^15",
    "redux": "^4"
}
```

Every plugin we create for Rematch must include Redux and @rematch/core as a peer dependency. Peer dependencies are basically the dependencies that our library/package needs to work but we don't want to ship them inside our library. We let the user install them in their code base. This brings flexibility for library consumers to use their own version of the required dependency.

As we're going to test that everything runs smoothly, we can install them as dev dependencies:

```
yarn add --dev @rematch/core prop-types redux
```

This command will install these dependencies just for development and won't impact our bundle size; these development dependencies are useful for making the tests more reliable since we'll test how our end users consume this library.

In the next section, we'll start programming our plugin step by step, introducing a new property to Rematch's models and a cache for improving the performance of our plugin.

Creating our plugin

Creating a Rematch plugin is as easy as creating an object with some properties, as you'll remember from *Chapter 8, The Rematch Plugins Ecosystem*. Rematch plugins accept certain properties; in this chapter, we're going to use two of them: onModel and createMiddleware.

onModel

The onModel hook is executed when the whole setup for the model is completed, that is, when the reducers and dispatchers are correctly injected and ready to use. The onModel hook is executed for each model, allowing us to pick or overwrite values from any model.

In our case, we want to save a cache of each typings property of each model. This is a required step for our plugin because we'll need to access these typings properties later to use the plugin in the createMiddleware hook.

Let's next add to the exposed property a new property called onModel:

```
onModel: (model) => {
  TYPINGS_CACHE[model.name] = model.typings;
}
```

The TYPINGS_CACHE variable is a new constant that we created outside of the createTypedStatePlugin function. Keeping this variable outside of the function context makes the typings values persistent and faster to access:

```
const TYPINGS_CACHE = {};
function createTypedStatePlugin() {
```

Now, we'll have inside this TYPINGS_CACHE constant every model typings property referenced by its model's name. So basically, to access any value, we'll need the model's name.

createMiddleware

To conclude with our plugin implementation, we need the last part of the plugin. After the onModel property, we can add the createMiddleware property:

```
createMiddleware: () => (store) => (next) => (action) => {
  const called = next(action);
  const [modelName] = action.type.split("/");
  const typings = TYPINGS_CACHE[modelName];

  if (typings) {
    const payload = store.getState()[modelName];
    validate(typings, payload, modelName);
  }

  return called;
},
```

In this code snippet, we're destructuring the action argument. As you'll remember, whenever a Rematch model dispatches any action, it follows this convention:

```
{
  "type": "modelName/action",
  "payload": {}
}
```

So, basically, in the second line, we're splitting our `action.type` property by the slash character, which is giving us access to the actual model name. As a consequence, we have direct access to the `typings` values we saved previously in the `onModel` hook.

If `typings` value is not null, means that model has an schema to compare against, to compare the schema with the dispatched payload we use the `validate` function with the corresponding typings of the model dispatched, the payload dispatched and the model's name for improving the verbosity of the error message in the case of any error occurring.

To implement the `validate` method, we're going to use a library called `prop-types` (`https://github.com/facebook/prop-types`). If you're used to developing with React, you'll be used to hearing about the `prop-types` library, because it's the official runtime type checking library for React props and similar objects.

This small library (897 bytes when minified) exposes practically any JavaScript primitive value, as in the following example:

```
MyComponent.propTypes = {
  optionalArray: PropTypes.array,
  optionalBool: PropTypes.bool,
}
```

Or you can even mark property values as required:

```
MyComponent.propTypes = {
  requiredArray: PropTypes.array.isRequired,
  requiredBool: PropTypes.bool.isRequired,
}
```

So, how are we going to use this library? Basically, we expect that our models will contain something similar to this. Imagine a state with a property name, which is a string, and an age, which is a number:

```
state: {
  name: "Sergio",
  age: 23,
},
```

This could easily be a state of any of our models, so to type this, we would include a new property called `typings` with the corresponding `prop-types` primitives:

```
import T from "prop-types";


const model = {
  state: {
    name: "Sergio",
    age: 23,
  },
  typings: {
    name: T.string.isRequired,
    age: T.number.isRequired,
  }
}
```

Given this model with this `typings`, when any action passed to this model passes `undefined` or `null` in any of these two properties, it will make the plugin log a warning.

This logic can be implemented inside this `validate()` function:

```
import PROP_TYPES_SECRET from "prop-types/lib/
ReactPropTypesSecret";
function validate(typeSpecs, payload, modelName) {
  for (const key in typeSpecs) {
    if (typeSpecs[key]) {
      const error = typeSpecs[key] (
        payload,
        key,
        modelName,
        "property",
        null,
        PROP_TYPES_SECRET
      );

      if (error instanceof Error) {
        console.warn(`[Rematch]: ${error.message}`);
      }
```

```
        }
      }
    }
```

This function is just iterating through the typeSpecs object, which is the first argument that contains an object of prop-types schemas, the ones that the user defined in their models. The second argument is the payload, used to compare the expected primitive defined in the typeSpecs object against the primitive value of the payload, and to finish, modelName is used to give context to the error response.

The rest of the parameters are required by the prop-types library to improve the logging message. We pass property to improve the error message. null is the component name but as we're not using React components, we can pass it as null, and to finish, we pass PROP_TYPES_SECRET, which is something internal that the React prop-types team added to make sure that the executor is safe.

In the case of returning an error, we'll log a warning in our console. This could throw an error or do any cool idea that you can imagine, such as sending these errors to an error-reporting application.

Our plugin is ready, and everything should work fine, but how do we know that this plugin is going to work fine in a Rematch application?

In the next section, we'll create some integration tests where we'll use this plugin in a Rematch store and test some scenarios, such as dispatching an action with multiple errors.

Testing our plugin

Tsdx creates all the configuration we need to make our tests with Jest out of the box. As you'll remember, we used this testing framework for our Amazhop application. We'll just use the same approach.

Inside our index.test.ts file, we can add a describe() function that describes what we are going to test:

```
describe("Rematch Plugin Typed State", () => {})
```

Since we're going to use the same model in every test, we can create a constant to extend a base model for each test:

```
const BASE_MODEL = {
  name: 'user',
  state: {
    name: "Sergio",
    age: 23,
  },

  reducers: {
    update: (_, { name, age }) => ({
      name,
      age,
    }),
  },
};
```

This code is a basic Rematch model, a state with one string and one number, and a reducer to update these values. We'll use this BASE_MODEL constant to create a different typings property in each test.

To get started testing our plugin, we can test the scenario where we dispatch a reducer with an invalid payload. First, we need to mock the console.warn method. We're going to mock it to be able to intercept the results returned from the plugin:

```
it("should throw a warning when one type is invalid", () => {
  globalThis.console.warn = jest.fn();
```

The globalThis property contains the global this value. The main reason to use globalThis is that historically, accessing the global object required so many syntaxes depending on the environment. For example, on websites, we could use window or self but in Node.js, none of that works, so you would have to use global. Using globalThis provides a standard way of accessing the this value.

Jest.fn() is the official function that Jest offers for mocking functions. We can replace any of our internal code with jest.fn() and test against that mocked function. We can use this function to check if the function has been called or not, and even check with what arguments has been called the function.

Now, we can extend the user model with the corresponding `typings` schema:

```
const user = {
  ...BASE_MODEL,
  typings: {
    name: T.string.isRequired,
    age: T.number.isRequired,
  },
};
```

This code is spreading into a new object, our BASE_MODEL object, with a new `typings` property. The `typings` property contains the shape of our state and the properties that are required. If we try to update these properties to `null` or `undefined`, we'll see a `console.warn` message in our console.

Let's initialize the store with `createTypedStatePlugin()` and dispatch the reducer with the wrong properties. In this case, we're setting name as `undefined`:

```
const { dispatch } = init({
  models: { user },
  plugins: [createTypedStatePlugin()],
});


dispatch.user.update({ name: undefined, age: 26 });
```

If we run the testing suite, by running `yarn test`, we'll see that our test passes and no logs appear in our terminal. This is because we mocked the `globalThis.console.warn` method, to be able to expect which text will be returned and how many times:

```
expect(globalThis.console.warn).toHaveBeenCalledTimes(1);
expect(globalThis.console.warn).toHaveBeenCalledWith(
  "[Rematch]: The property `name` is marked as required in
  `user`, but its value is `undefined`."
);
```

These tests will pass, and we checked that the error is self-explanatory. We're dispatching the property name as `undefined`, and the plugin is warning us that this property is required.

But what about when we dispatch an action where the entire payload is wrong? We should see two errors in our console, right?

We can create another test that dispatches an entirely wrong payload, for instance, `name` as `undefined` and `age` as a string when it should be a number:

```
dispatch.user.update({ name: undefined, age: "26" });
expect(globalThis.console.warn).toHaveBeenCalledTimes(2);
expect(globalThis.console.warn).toHaveBeenNthCalledWith(
    1,
    "[Rematch]: The property `name` is marked as required in
    `user`, but its value is `undefined`."
);
expect(globalThis.console.warn).toHaveBeenNthCalledWith(
    2,
    "[Rematch]: Invalid property `age` of type `string` supplied
    to `user`, expected `number`."
);
```

In this code, we're expecting `console.warn` to have been called two times, and then we check which messages are returned in the first call and the second call.

This plugin works perfectly; we tested it inside a real Rematch store in the same way that our users will use it, but there's still one thing left to do.

In the next section, we'll see how we can use this module in any Rematch application without publishing it to NPM using symlinks to make sure that everything runs fine before we finish the chapter by publishing the library to NPM.

Publishing to NPM

What's a symbolic link? It's a kind of file, normally hidden from us, that points to another file, much like a shortcut.

The main purpose of using **symbolic links**, or **symlinks**, is that we can link a local dependency and use it in another project. This is useful for developing new libraries or packages where we can test them in real projects.

Both Yarn and NPM can be used to make symbolic links with just one command:

```
~: yarn link
~: npm link
```

Taking the code we implemented in this chapter, in the root of our project, we can execute the yarn link command:

```
~: yarn link
yarn link v1.22.10
success Registered "typed-state-plugin".
info You can now run `yarn link "typed-state-plugin"` in the
projects where you want to use this package and it will be used
instead.
  Done in 0.07s
```

Magically, we'll get a symbolic link of the entire code base where we implemented the plugin and it is ready to use in our Amazhop applications. But remember, this is only for development. To use it in production, the bundle should be published to NPM.

Access the Amazhop application and execute the following command:

```
yarn link "typed-state-plugin"
```

Now, you can just import the plugin as a normal dependency:

```
import createTypedStatePlugin from "typed-state-plugin";

export const store = init({
  models: { shop, cart },
  redux: {
    rootReducers: {
      RESET: () => undefined,
    },
  },
  plugins: [
    createTypedStatePlugin(),
```

For instance, you can type the shop state like this to force an error when we dispatch a Boolean value:

```
typings: {
  query: T.string.isRequired,
},
```

This will log a warning in our console tools when we launch the application using `yarn dev` as usual:

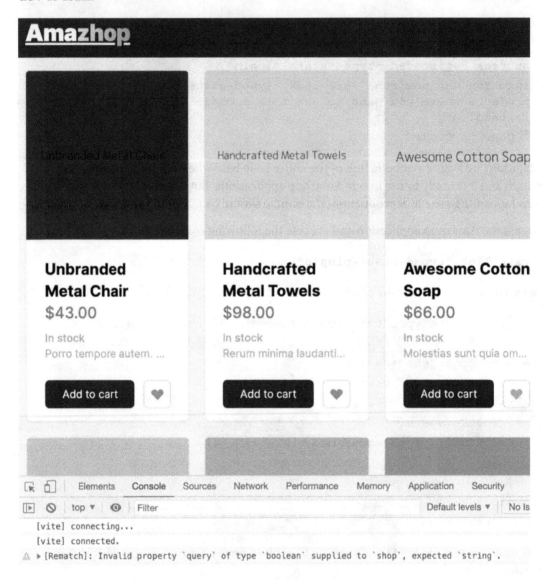

Figure 9.1 – Amazhop warning with the typed-state plugin

We can check whether our application is logging the expected behavior correctly, but how can we publish this package to make it usable for everyone?

We just need two commands:

```
yarn build
npm publish
```

The yarn build command will create a dist/ folder with all the required modules to make it work in any environment, and also Tsdx pre-configured our package.json to make npm publish one command.

Make sure that the name property inside the package.json is unique. If you try to deploy your library with the name @rematch/typed-state, it will fail.

The npm publish command is the official command that NPM offers for publishing packages to the public registry. Publishing the package with this command will create a page on the official NPM website to make it installable through NPM or Yarn itself: https://www.npmjs.com/package/@rematch/typed-state.

Also, it makes the package public for everyone, allowing us to install the package in our application and build it for production:

```
yarn add @rematch/typed-state
```

This command will install the package correctly in any application, making it usable for everyone.

We saw that creating and extending our requirements with Rematch's plugins is easy, fast, and safe. It is easy because the Rematch API is very clear, and after this chapter, you should see how Rematch's plugins can extend functionality easily. It is fast because we don't need to set up anything; we just use Tsdx, write our index file, and we are ready to publish. It is safe because Rematch can be easily tested with any JavaScript testing framework.

Summary

In this chapter, we have learned how we can create from scratch any JavaScript library and how tools such as Tsdx can help us to have an easier development experience. Also, we saw a little introduction to TypeScript, and how Rematch plugins are easily created and integrated into existing code bases.

In the next chapter, we'll migrate our entire Amazhop web application to TypeScript, focusing on Rematch TypeScript helpers, which will help us to create a complete typed Rematch store with autocomplete for every reducer, effect, and even our state.

10
Rewrite a Full Code Base from JavaScript to TypeScript

In this chapter, we'll learn how **TypeScript** development experience is fascinating and how it makes a plain language such as JavaScript a language for every use case. We will also learn how Rematch takes TypeScript static types and makes a complete typed system, giving us the confidence to refactor our applications or websites easily. We'll discover how TypeScript makes the development experience of Rematch and React a pleasure and how easy it is to introduce business logic into our Rematch views using the typing system.

In this chapter, we'll cover the following topics:

- Introduction to TypeScript
- Rematch utility types
- Converting Rematch models to TypeScript
- TypeScript with React and Rematch

By the end of the chapter, you will understand how Rematch with TypeScript is one of the best decisions we can make when building a new product and how Rematch exposes some interesting utility types for archiving a complete typed code base.

Technical requirements

To follow along with this chapter, you will need the following:

- Basic knowledge of **Vanilla JavaScript** and **ES6** features
- Basic knowledge of **TypeScript**
- Basic knowledge of **HTML5** features
- **Node.js 12** or later installed
- Basic knowledge of **React** and **CSS**
- A browser (**Chrome** or **Firefox**, for instance)
- A code editor (**Visual Studio Code**, for instance)

You can find the code for this chapter in the book's GitHub repo: `https://github.com/PacktPublishing/Redux-Made-Easy-with-Rematch/tree/main/packages/chapter-10`.

This chapter assumes that you know a bit about TypeScript, and that you're familiar with the TypeScript ecosystem and which problems it tries to solve. But just in case, we'll do a brief introduction to what TypeScript is, along with the how and why.

Introduction to TypeScript

TypeScript is an open source language that builds on JavaScript, meaning all valid JavaScript code is also TypeScript code. It allows us to write types of objects, variables, or functions, providing better documentation and allowing TypeScript to validate the fact that our code is working as expected, but writing types is purely optional since TypeScript has type inference and, most of the time, TypeScript will know which type a constant is by its value.

When we're using plain JavaScript and we're developing a website with a lot of variables, sometimes, we try to access methods of our variables that don't exist.

For instance, when accessing `.toLowerCase()` of a number variable:

```
const value = 10_000
console.log(value.toLowerCase())
```

This code in our development editor won't log an error, or we won't see any change in our code. But let's say we try to run this code:

```
> value.toLowerCase()
Uncaught TypeError: value.toLowerCase is not a function
```

When JavaScript is executed, it returns an uncaught type error, an error that didn't appear while we were writing our code in our development editor but it failed on execution. TypeScript solves this inference problem with a typing system and, of course, an improved inference system giving us some IntelliSense about which functions, accessors, and setters exist in our variables.

This file, instead of being just a JavaScript file, is a TypeScript file, with the extension basically renamed from to `.js` to `.ts`:

```
const value = 10_000

value.toLowerCase()    Property 'toLowerCase' does not exist on type '10000'.
```

Figure 10.1 – Visual Studio Code showing TypeScript errors

TypeScript is warning us that the `.toLowerCase()` property doesn't exist on type `10000`, because `value` is a number, and `.toLowerCase()` method doesn't exist on number values. It knows that it doesn't exist because it automatically infers the value defined. If quotation marks are inserted around the `10_000` value, it will know that it is a string.

But what about complex data structures? How does it know when we receive data coming from an API response? That is easy; just type the `return` type of the function:

```
type ComplexStructure = { image_url: string }
async function simulatedApiResponse():
Promise<ComplexStructure> {
  return {
    image_url: ""
  }
}
```

This use case is a common scenario where we submit requests to a backend service and a response is returned. Since TypeScript is not evaluated on runtime, which is basically a static type checker, this makes it impossible to infer which data will be returned from that request, which is why we need to sometimes use the types that TypeScript offers.

TypeScript documentation is a masterpiece in terms of how something should be documented and oriented, which is why I encourage you to read `https://www.typescriptlang.org`, you will see a lot of examples explaining how TypeScript works and which types you can use.

But before starting on Rematch utility types, I want to introduce a subsection of TypeScript: **generics**.

Generics

TypeScript generics are one of the most important features of Rematch because this typing system is really based on it and its utility types expect to use them.

Basically, we can create types that accept any type of types – that's what *generic* means, right?

Let's look at an example. We create a function, called `identity(arg)`, which could be multiple things. The easiest way is to type it like this:

```
function identity(arg: any): any {
   return arg;
}
```

This will work and is certainly generic, but it will cause the function to accept all types for the `arg` argument, losing all the information about what the type was when the function returns.

Instead, we need a way to capture the type of argument – this is where TypeScript generics come in. We define a generic type, which will be tracked along with the static checking, and will determine which type it is:

```
function identity<Type>(arg: Type): Type {
   return arg;
}

identity("string")
identity(10)
```

And of course, it accepts any complex type, so you can pass an argument type to the function:

```
type ComplexStructure = { image_url: string }
identity<ComplexStructure>({ image_url: '' })
```

With these concepts clear, we can now jump into Rematch and the TypeScript ecosystem, where we will discover which utility types are exported from the Rematch library and how we can get autocomplete and inference of our Rematch's models and state.

Rematch utility types

Since version 2 of Rematch, which was released on February 1, 2020, it is fully compatible out of the box with TypeScript. There are some key concepts that are important to understand in terms of how Rematch makes it possible to type every corner of our state.

We will start with the first one we should create when creating a Rematch application with TypeScript.

RootModel

`RootModel`, or whatever you want to call this interface, is the main interface of our store. It's a TypeScript interface that stores all of our model's types:

```
import { Models } from '@rematch/core'
import { count } from './models/count'

export interface RootModel extends Models<RootModel> {
    count: typeof count
}
export const models: RootModel = { count }
```

We need to create a circular cycle where `RootModel` is injected as a generic type into the `Models` type because Rematch architecture and how it's designed makes it possible to access state and dispatch effects or reducers from other models. Therefore, we need to make each model of our store available to TypeScript in some way.

`RootModel` will be the main generic type for the incoming sections, which, given a scenario, will extract the desired values.

init<RootModel, ExtraModels>()

The Rematch `init()` function in TypeScript accepts two generics. This is because when we were designing the TypeScript API, we wanted to use a single `RootModel` argument and get the type info of each model inside the `models` config, but TypeScript has a design limitation related to partial type inference that made it impossible to merge `RootModel` and `ExtraModels` together. That's the reason why we use one type to define our local models and another to define the plugin ones.

To get started with the most basic method of Rematch, that is the `init()` function, we must understand what `RootModel` and `ExtraModels` are.

RootModel

The first type argument that the `init()` function accepts is the `RootModel` interface we created previously. It is fundamental to get a fully typed store since it returns a Rematch store instance completely typed. Even Rematch plugins are fully typed:

```
import { init } from '@rematch/core'
import { RootModel, models } from './models'

export const store = init<RootModel>({
  models,
})
```

This code snippet is a demonstration of how you can pass the `RootModel` generic to the `init()` function, which will automatically type the store returned.

ExtraModels

The second argument is optional and, as the name indicates, is used to pass any additional models that may be injected through plugins such as `@rematch/loading` or `@rematch/updated`:

```
import { init } from "@rematch/core";
import createLoadingPlugin, { ExtraModelsFromLoading } from "@rematch/loading";
import { shop, cart, RootModel } from "./models";

type FullModel = ExtraModelsFromLoading<RootModel>;

export const store = init<RootModel, FullModel>({
  models: { shop, cart },
  plugins: [
    createLoadingPlugin(),
  ],
});
```

The Rematch loading and Rematch updated plugins use named exports to export `ExtraModelsFromLoading` and `ExtraModelsFromUpdates`, respectively. To pass the types generated by this utility type to the `init()` function, we need to do this because loading and updated plugins create models dynamically when the plugin initializes and their state is accessible, in the same way as our standard models.

We can extend the `FullModel` type as much as we can. Imagine we have a scenario with loading and updated plugins together; we could just use the & operator:

```
type FullModel = ExtraModelsFromLoading<RootModel> &
ExtraModelsFromUpdated<RootModel>;
export const store = init<RootModel, FullModel>({
```

Thanks to this, we can make Rematch plugins totally extensible thanks to TypeScript modularity. Any plugin can extend this utility type and any application with Rematch could use them.

createModel

`createModel` is the utility type responsible for typing and inferring our Rematch models correctly:

```
import { createModel } from "@rematch/core";
```

Basically, this is a utility type for achieving the automatic inferring of some parameters that Rematch models expose, such as the root state, which will be automatically inferred and we don't need to type it.

Let's now check how this works with the help of a simple example:

```
export const shop = {
  state: {},
  reducers: {},
  effects: (dispatch) => ({})
}
```

This is just an empty Rematch model. Let's now introduce the `createModel()` utility type:

```
export const shop = createModel<RootModel>()({
  state: {},
  reducers: {},
  effects: (dispatch) => ({})
})
```

We just need to pass the `RootModel` type to the `createModel` generic type, and then use the **currying** workaround. Currying basically splits a single generic function of two type parameters into two curried functions of one type of parameter each:

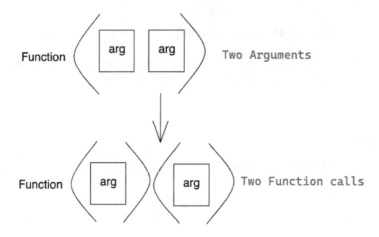

Figure 10.2 – Function currying technique

In our case the first function argument is empty and is used for specifying the generic type, and the other one is used to pass the Rematch model that will be auto inferred by TypeScript.

This is a really common problem in these kinds of scenarios since it is a TypeScript design limitation that doesn't support partial type parameter inference, at least for now. That is the reason for using double parentheses – because we can't specify internally in Rematch which parameters should be inferred by TypeScript and which ones should be taken from the `RootModel` type.

Automatically, since we add the `RootModel` generic to the `createModel` function, every `state` and `rootState` parameter of our reducers and effects will be inferred, and also the dispatch function passed through the first argument of the `effects` property will be typed with all our methods that we can dispatch.

However, you may be asking yourself, how do we type our state when it contains complex structures, such as arrays, with complex objects inside? We can do two things:

- Use the `as` keyword: TypeScript accepts writing the `as` keyword to tell the compiler to consider the object as a type other than the type the compiler infers the object to be (this is called **Type Assertion**):

```
type ShopState = {
  products: Array<ProductType>;
```

```
    currentPage: number;
    totalCount: number;
    query: string | boolean;
};
export const shop = createModel<RootModel>()({
    state: {
        products: [],
        currentPage: 1,
        totalCount: 0,
        query: "",
    } as ShopState,
```

- Create your state object outside of the `createModel` function and type it like a common object: Automatically, TypeScript and Rematch will know how to infer that object:

```
type ShopState = {
    products: Array<ProductType>;
    currentPage: number;
    totalCount: number;
    query: string | boolean;
};


const SHOP_STATE_TYPED: ShopState = {
    products: [],
    currentPage: 1,
    totalCount: 0,
    query: "",
};
export const shop = createModel<RootModel>()({
    state: SHOP_STATE_TYPED,
```

Personally, I prefer the second choice a bit more than the first one, since the `SHOP_STATE_TYPED` constant could be exported for using it inside tests, and feels more readable to me, but any of these choices are valid and will work perfectly fine for Rematch and TypeScript.

RematchRootState

The `RematchRootState<RootModel>` utility type is useful for getting the IntelliSense of each model's state.

We'll use it when we have to type some Redux hooks such as `useDispatch`, or custom functions where we pass the entire root state and they are external to Rematch.

For example, given a function that filters by name and where the first parameter is `RematchRootState`, we can type it as follows:

```
export const filterByName = (
  rootState: RematchRootState<RootModel>,
  query: string
) =>
  rootState.shop.products.filter((product) =>
    product.productName.toLowerCase().includes(
    query.toLowerCase())
  );
```

By typing the `rootState` parameter, we'll get automatic IntelliSense of which models and which state values we can access, and also whether they may be undefined or null values, and even whether they're complex structures. Here, in this example where products are a complex type, we get the definition of our state type.

```
export const filterByName = (
  rootState: RematchRootState<RootModel>,
  query: string
) ⇒                         (property) products: ProductType[]
  rootState.shop.products.filter((product) ⇒
```

Figure 10.3 – Visual Studio Code IntelliSense of the RematchRootState utility type

In the internal typing system that makes this amazing experience possible, the `RematchRootState` utility type is heavily used, so it's safe to use it since it is battle-hardened.

RematchDispatch

`RematchDispatch<RootModel>` works in the same way as `RematchRootState<RootModel>`. Basically, they accept as generic the `RootModel` interface we named previously.

The principal function of `RematchDispatch<RootModel>` is to return which reducers and effects are available to dispatch, and the most important benefit is that `RematchDispatch` also types the payload we pass through the `dispatch` function, so basically, if we pass something that is incorrect, our TypeScript checker will warn us before our code runs at runtime.

Remember that we created a plugin in *Chapter 9, Composable Plugins - Create Your First Plugin*, with a similar feature, but for runtime instead of static-type checking as TypeScript does.

For example, we typed that the ADD_TO_CART reducer should receive at least the id property, which is a string and can't be null or undefined:

```
dispatch.cart.ADD_TO_CART({ id: null });    Type 'null' is not assignable to type 'string'.
dispatch.cart.ADD_TO_CART({ id: 1000 });    Type 'number' is not assignable to type 'string'.
```

Figure 10.4 – Visual Studio Code showing errors when trying to dispatch incorrect values

Automatically, we're seeing errors when we try to use the dispatch function with the wrong payload. This saves a lot of potential bugs and is one of the biggest benefits of using TypeScript. We get notified before our code runs that this code probably won't work correctly.

In the next section, we're going to put all this theory into practice by migrating our Amazhop application to TypeScript. This task sometimes takes a few months for big companies to do, but I'll give some hints on how to do it easily and gradually.

Converting Rematch models to TypeScript

To get started on migrating our project to TypeScript, we'll need some steps that will be common for any project:

- Create a configuration file for TypeScript.
- Rename files to TypeScript files.
- Installing declaration files and TypeScript dev dependency.

These steps will largely be required on all the projects you create with TypeScript, even without using Rematch. In this chapter, we won't explain every type we need to add to make the migration complete since it would become larger than desired. You can look at the result in the GitHub repository of the book, and you could also read the official TypeScript documentation regarding how to migrate from a JavaScript code base: `https://www.typescriptlang.org/docs/handbook/migrating-from-javascript.html`.

Creating the configuration file

Let's get started by creating a configuration file. We just need to create a `tsconfig.json` file in the root of our project with the following content:

```json
{
  "compilerOptions": {
    "target": "ESNext",
    "module": "ESNext",
    "lib": ["DOM", "DOM.Iterable", "ESNext"],
    "moduleResolution": "Node",
    "skipLibCheck": true,
    "esModuleInterop": true,
    "strict": true,
    "resolveJsonModule": true,
    "isolatedModules": true,
    "noEmit": true,
    "jsx": "react"
  },
  "include": ["./src", "./test"]
}
```

This is a configuration file for TypeScript. It's the most common `tsconfig.json` file when using TypeScript with Vite. You can take a look at the official TypeScript documentation to know more about each property:

https://www.typescriptlang.org/docs/handbook/tsconfig-json.html.

Renaming our files

To rename our files, we could just rename them manually, file by file, but sometimes, on larger projects, this task becomes tedious, so you can use this shell script instead:

```
find src/ test/ -type f \( -iname '*.js' -or -iname '*.jsx' \)
-not -wholename '*node_modules*' -exec sh -c 'mv "$1" `sed -Ee
"s/\.js(x)?$/\.ts\1/g" <<< "$1"`' _ {} \;
```

This script basically finds all the files inside the `src/` and `test/` folders that end with `.js` and rewrites them to `.ts`. The React JavaScript files, `.jsx`, are replaced by TypeScript React files, `.tsx`.

With these steps complete, we have already achieved a lot of early benefits, since our code editor is already displaying some code completion. TypeScript is probably already preventing us from realizing some bugs, such as forgetting to return at the end of a function or warning us about unreachable code or switch cases without the default case.

Installing declaration files

To get officially started with TypeScript in our code base, we need to install TypeScript as a development dependency. It isn't a dependency because TypeScript doesn't include any change in our bundle size with the typing since it is removed when Vite bundles our application because TypeScript is just a static type checker:

```
yarn add --dev typescript
```

Many of our dependencies will include their types published in the bundle of the library (Rematch does that), but also many of them use the GitHub repository, https://github.com/DefinitelyTyped/DefinitelyTyped. To type these libraries, the most famous case is React, which ships these types through the @types/react and @types/react-dom packages, respectively.

To achieve autocompletion and the advantages afforded by TypeScript's super-powers, we must install the following packages as development dependencies:

```
yarn add --dev @types/react @types/react-dom
```

Now we're ready to migrate our Rematch models to TypeScript, as we saw previously in our *Rematch utility types* section. We will begin with the RootModel interface, which should contain all the Rematch models of our store.

Creating the RootModel interface

Modify the src/store/models/index.ts file and include this new interface:

```
import type { Models } from "@rematch/core";
import { shop } from "./shop";
import { cart } from "./cart";


export interface RootModel extends Models<RootModel> {
  shop: typeof shop;
  cart: typeof cart;
}
export { shop, cart };
```

The `RootModel` interface is the most frequently used type in development with Rematch since it contains all the shapes of our Rematch models and makes them available in other models.

Now, we can modify our models with the Rematch utility function called `createModel`.

Using createModel in a Rematch model

To get started with the `createModel` function, we can check that the `state` argument in our reducers isn't typed. Basically, TypeScript throws an error, reporting to us the fact that `state` property has an implicit `any` type. This is because we're not yet using the `createModel` function. It has the responsibility of auto-inferring and typing our Rematch models efficiently:

```
export const shop = {
  state: {
    products: [],
    currentPage: 1,
    totalCount: 0,
    query: "",
  },
  reducers: {
    SET_PRODUCTS(
      state,      Parameter 'state' implicitly has an 'any' type.
      {
        products,
        totalCount,
```

Figure 10.5 – Rematch model throwing TypeScript errors

The `createModel` function will automatically type these arguments, and will also type the `dispatch` argument in the `effects` property, and of course the `rootState` argument in `effects`.

This is going to be resolved easily. Let's start by importing the `createModel` utility type along with `RootModel` from our `index.ts` file:

```
import { createModel } from "@rematch/core";
import type { RootModel } from "./index";
```

Now, we must pass the object model to the curried function:

```
export const shop = createModel<RootModel>()({
```

Automatically, after this simple change, we won't get any errors pertaining to state. This is because, under the hood, `createModel` is typing these arguments.

As you can see in the following screenshot, our `state` argument is partially correctly inferred:

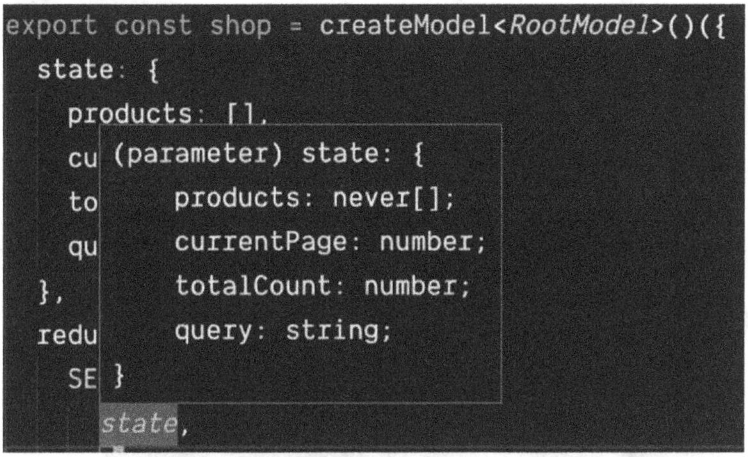

Figure 10.6 – Rematch createModel typing the state argument

However, there is still work to do if we want a fully typed model. As you can see, `currentPage`, `totalCount`, and `query` are correctly inferred since their values are simply primitives, but `products` is a complex array with a custom object. We can type this just by creating a new type and adding an `as` property to the state.

Let's start by creating the type for our product, since `products` is an array of products:

```
export type ProductType = {
  id: string;
  image_url: string;
  stock: number;
  price: number;
  productName: string;
  productDescription: string;
  favorite: boolean;
};
```

This is a simple type describing the structure of any product. If you're not familiar with TypeScript, basically, TypeScript types define the shape of objects or arrays with primitive types that come out of the box with TypeScript, such as `string`, `boolean`, or `number`.

Now, just create a new type called `ShopState`:

```
export type ShopState = {
  products: Array<ProductType>;
  currentPage: number;
  totalCount: number;
  query: string | boolean;
};
```

This state type will be used with the `as` keyword to describe the state's shape:

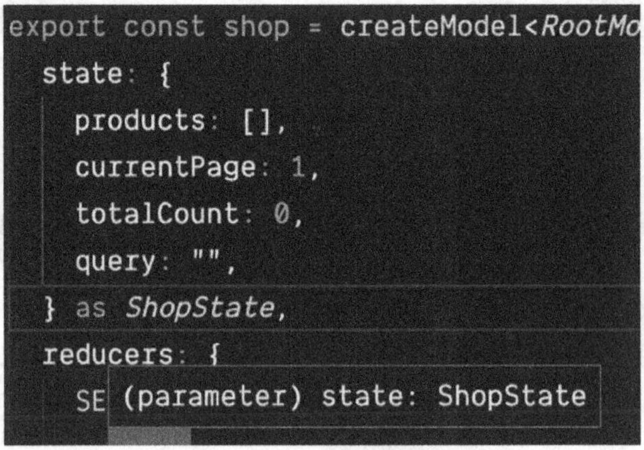

```
export const shop = createModel<RootMo
  state: {
    products: [],
    currentPage: 1,
    totalCount: 0,
    query: "",
  } as ShopState,
  reducers: {
    SE (parameter) state: ShopState
```

Figure 10.7 – The state argument inferred as ShopState instead of never[]

As you can check, automatically we're getting our `state` argument inferred thanks to the `as` operator, and any reducer we write, or any effect, will be auto-completed with this shape. If we try to modify, delete, or add any existing property, this will result in TypeScript failing to warn us about the fact that property x doesn't exist in `ShopState`.

Just with this, we're already much safer than we were initially with just JavaScript, and we're getting autocompletion and warnings about a lot of uncovered sections of our project, but there's still a hole in our effects and reducers: our payloads are not typed since they could be anything. Let's type them.

Making payloads fully typed

For example, taking this reducer of the shop state, SET_PRODUCTS expects an object payload with products and totalCount, and right now it's inferred as any, but what if we just type it to an exact thing:

```
SET_PRODUCTS(state, { products, totalCount } : {
  products: Array<ProductType>,
  totalCount: number
}) {
```

This is basically defining the fact that this payload argument will just accept a products array of ProductType, and totalCount as number. This becomes super useful when using Rematch in our views since we'll get an auto-completion of what the reducer expects, or the effect to receive, and, of course, warnings if we pass something that's not expected.

These techniques are common in every Rematch model. Give it a try and you will see how easy it is to modify our Rematch models to be compatible with TypeScript.

There's just one thing left before moving to React views: passing RootModel to our init() function. To do this, modify the src/store/index.ts file with these new types:

```
import createLoadingPlugin, { ExtraModelsFromLoading } from "@
rematch/loading";
import { shop, cart, RootModel } from "./models";


type FullModel = ExtraModelsFromLoading<RootModel>;


export const store = init<RootModel, FullModel>({
```

Since @rematch/loading creates a new model dynamically, we must use the utility type, which exports the plugin. ExtraModelsFromLoading basically makes it available under the hood, loading the state in any model or view.

Personally, I like to export two types into this file, which are heavily used along with the project:

```
export type Dispatch = RematchDispatch<RootModel>;
export type RootState = RematchRootState<RootModel, FullModel>;
```

These are the utility types that Rematch exports, but with the arguments already filled since we're importing `RootModel` and `FullModel` into this file. If we need to use these types somewhere, we just need to import `Dispatch` and not `RematchDispatch` and `RootModel` independently.

Now, we're ready to move on to our React view. The react-redux library is compatible out of the box with Rematch and, of course, with TypeScript.

TypeScript with React and Rematch

Thanks to TypeScript, we're now able to know which state is accessible, possibly undefined, or even doesn't exist. We just need to tweak some of the functions that we were already using, such as `useDispatch` or `useSelector`.

Taking `src/components/Cart` as an example, let's check how Rematch makes it extremely easy to power our React views with TypeScript IntelliSense:

```
import type { RootState, Dispatch } from "../../store";

export const Cart = () => {
  const dispatch = useDispatch<Dispatch>();
  const quantityById = useSelector(
    (rootState: RootState) => rootState.cart.quantityById
  );
  const cartProducts = useSelector(store.select.cart.
  getCartProducts);
  const totalPrice = useSelector(store.select.cart.total);
```

As we saw previously, TypeScript generics are important for Rematch and also for React and Redux, since we can pass our `RematchDispatch` type, exported as `Dispatch`, to the `useDispatch` hook. This gives us a complete typed dispatch method.

We can check this by trying to pass any argument to the `RESTORE_CART` reducer. TypeScript warns that this reducer doesn't accept any arguments:

```
<button                          (method) RESTORE_CART(): Action<void, void>
  onClick={() => dispatch.cart.RESTORE_CART("try")}    Expected 0 arguments, but got 1
```

Figure 10.8 – TypeScript warning with the Rematch TypeScript dispatcher

Also, we use the `RootState` type to type the `useSelector` `rootState` argument. If we try to access any value that doesn't exist, this selector will fail.

And incredibly, our Rematch selectors are automatically inferred under the hood thanks to the Rematch typing system. Automatically, the `useSelector` hook will know what the `getCartProducts` selector returns.

This makes it super easy to follow how our state flows in our views, and easy to refactor when we add, remove, or modify any new property that is required or optional. For instance, we automatically get an autocompletion of our array of `ProductType`:

```
cartProducts.map(
  (product) =>
    product && (
      <CartProduct
        key={product.id}
        product={product.|    Parsing error: Identifier expected
        quantity={quantit ⊗ favorite
      />             ⊗ id
    )              ⊗ image_url
  )              ⊗ price
) : (             ⊗ productDescription
  <div className="text-cent ⊗ productName
    <h5 className="font-med ⊗ stock
```

Figure 10.9 – Visual Studio Code IntelliSense with Rematch TypeScript

Visual Studio Code automatically displays a popup of which keys are available to access, and if we try to access any that are not typed in our model, it will fail.

Introducing TypeScript to an existing project built with JavaScript can be a tedious task, but since TypeScript makes things easier by doing it gradually, we'll see even more adoption in the future with any JavaScript project created from the start with TypeScript since the development experience benefits from multiple advantages, such as spotting bugs early, predictability, readability, optional static typing, fast refactoring, and much more.

Since the v2 release of Rematch, as maintainers, we have largely focused our time investment on improving the TypeScript experience, and we ended with a library of less than 2 KB that offers an amazing development experience without any trade-offs.

Summary

In this chapter, we learned how to gradually adopt TypeScript with an existing code base built with React. We also learned how Rematch exports some utility types to make things easier and we reviewed how migrating a project to TypeScript gives us a lot of benefits that make the effort associated with migrating the project to TypeScript worthwhile.

In the next chapter, we are going to create a React Native application from scratch, which will be a shop application with a common data layer. This means that we're going to build an Amazhop application for Apple and Android that will share the data layer with the Amazhop website. Instead of writing two pieces of business logic, we're just going to share the Amazhop implementation through NPM modules.

11
Rematch with React Native and Expo – A Real-World Mobile App

In this chapter, we'll learn how to set up a Yarn workspace architecture from scratch, discovering their limitations and benefits and how they can solve unmaintainable large monolithic repositories. We'll discover where React and React Native differ and how Rematch and Redux make sharing business logic easy through distributable packages, making our application and website business logic fully shared.

In this chapter, we'll cover the following topics:

- Introduction to workspaces
- Setting up our workspace
- Creating distributable business logic
- Using the business logic in our Amazhop website
- Creating a React Native application with Expo

By the end of the chapter, you will know how to set up any Yarn or NPM monorepo architecture. Also, you will be able to create a package from scratch for distributing the business logic of Rematch and its types and, of course, you will have learned how building interfaces with React Native and Rematch is a pleasure.

Technical requirements

To follow along with this chapter, you will need the following:

- Basic knowledge of **Vanilla JavaScript** and **ES6** features

- Basic knowledge of **TypeScript**

- Basic knowledge of **React Native**

- **Node.js >= 12** installed

- Basic knowledge of **React** and **CSS**

- A browser (**Chrome** or **Firefox**, for instance)

- A code editor (**Visual Studio Code**, for instance)

You can find the code for this chapter in the book's GitHub repository:

- React Native application: `https://github.com/PacktPublishing/Redux-Made-Easy-with-Rematch/tree/main/packages/chapter-11`.

- Distributable business logic: `https://github.com/PacktPublishing/Redux-Made-Easy-with-Rematch/tree/main/packages/shared-logic`.

Introduction to workspaces

As you'll remember from *Chapter 9, Composable Plugins – Create Your First Plugin*, in the *Publishing to NPM* section, we used a computer machine technique called symbolic linking, which helped us to test our Rematch plugin on another code base without the requirement of publishing the package to NPM.

However, this situation sometimes gets harder because linking creates a symbolic link to our project folder, also to `node_modules`, and sometimes we get in trouble with duplicate dependencies, or, even worse, our symbolic link breaks our development environment.

Basically, in this book, we have forced the scenario of building the same application for the web and now mobile with React Native, but our application will have the same business logic, the same data layer, the same way of fetching and accessing the data: Rematch.

To handle this situation, we could just create a Git repository with our website and the business logic and another Git repository with our React Native application and another one for the Amazhop website repository. This means that if we change something in our website, we'll have to copy and paste these changes to the other repository. Complex, right?

Since Rematch is framework-agnostic, and Redux too, you can use Rematch anywhere – on React, React Native, Vue, Angular, Vanilla JavaScript… This introduces a new paradigm. What about building a module to create our business logic that will be shared through our websites or applications? Instead of maintaining two Rematch stores, we just maintain one.

This scenario, some years ago, was handled by creating a large monolithic code base, or by simply creating multiple repositories with complex continuous integrations and issues with testing as a whole.

Workspaces, also called **monorepos**, are a new way to configure our packages' architecture, basically allowing us to set up multiple packages in such a way that we only need to run `yarn install` once to install all of them in a single go. This converts our code base into small, encapsulated modules that can be reused anywhere inside our monorepo.

Monorepos have a large list of benefits but one of the most important ones is that running `yarn install` or `npm install` reduces redundancy considerably since most package managers employ hoisting schemas to extract and flatten all dependent modules as much as possible into a centralized location, normally `node_modules`. This means that if our package uses `@rematch/core` in multiple packages, it will just be installed once.

To understand this a bit more, let's explain this Yarn workspaces architecture diagram:

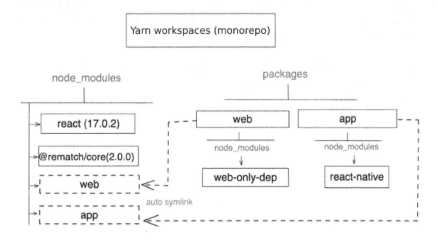

Figure 11.1 – Yarn workspaces hoisting architecture

This scenario is similar to what we are going to build in this chapter because we have the Amazhop website built throughout the book, and we're going to build a new React Native application with business logic shared with the website. This logic will be shared through Yarn workspaces.

Basically, dependencies that aren't used in another package are installed locally in that package folder, otherwise, they're hoisted to the root `node_modules` folder.

In *Figure 11.1*, **react** and **@rematch/core** are hoisted to the root `node_modules` folder since the **web** and **app** packages use that library, but the app that uses **react-native** is not hoisted because it isn't used elsewhere.

In the next section, we're going to create a Yarn workspaces architecture from scratch and we'll learn how to set up any workspace architecture for Yarn or NPM.

Setting up our workspace

If you followed this book's code in the official GitHub repository, you probably noticed that we had a file structure like this:

```
├── package.json
├── packages
│   ├── chapter-x
│   ├── chapter-y
└── yarn.lock
```

Workspaces are usually structured like this: a root `package.json` file and infinite modules inside a `packages/` folder. This module must contain a `package.json` file, which must have name and version properties.

It is flexible enough to allow us to define in the root `package.json` file where your modules are located. So, technically, you could just create the modules in the root, or even inside other folders or names.

For example, we could create a root `package.json` file with this configuration:

```
{
    "name": "my-workspaces-project",
    "version": "0.1.0",
    "private": true,
    "workspaces": [
```

```
        "public-modules/**",
    ]
}
```

When running, `yarn install` or `npm install` (remember, with Version 7) will automatically understand that you're using a monorepo architecture and it must also install the modules inside the `public-modules/` folder. You can install dependencies, or even development dependencies, in the root `package.json` file, and they will be available for every module you add to `public-modules/`.

With these concepts understood, we can move forward to create our own workspace or monorepo. Remember that we're already using this concept in the official GitHub repository of this book and also in the Rematch code base. Feel free to take a look.

Creating the workspace

To get started with a workspace, we just need to create a folder on our machine and add a `package.json` file with a property called `workspaces`. It's going to be an array of folders where our modules, websites, and packages exist.

Our workspace will contain these projects:

- **Amazhop website**: We'll copy the application we finished in *Chapter 10, Rewrite a Full Code Base from JavaScript to TypeScript*, and we'll make some adjustments to change our store to a shared one.

- **Amazhop React Native application**: We're going to use the **Expo CLI** to create a new React Native application with TypeScript.

- **Amazhop business logic**: We're going to create a new Tsdx module as we did in *Chapter 9, Composable Plugins – Create Your First Plugin*, with the Rematch Amazhop model's utility functions, to use it later in the app and on the web.

We have to create three folders inside our project, so let's get started:

```
mkdir rematch-workspace
cd rematch-workspace/
yarn init -y
```

These commands will create a folder called `rematch-workpace/` and a `package.json` file in the root of this package.

Let's adjust the `package.json` file to match the workspace specification:

```json
{
  "name": "rematch-workspace",
  "private": true,
  "version": "1.0.0",
  "main": "index.js",
  "author": "Sergio Moreno",
  "license": "MIT",
  "workspaces": [
    "packages/**"
  ]
}
```

We added the `workspaces` property and we're going to locate all our websites inside a `packages/` folder, so let's create these folders:

```
mkdir packages/
mkdir packages/web packages/app
```

Now that we have created all the folders, we need to get this workspace functional. We need to start moving pieces together.

In the next section, we'll go step by step, cloning our Amazhop web package into the workspace, extracting the shared logic to create the distributable business logic, and to conclude, we'll implement a React Native application with Expo.

Creating distributable business logic

In this section, we're going to clone our Amazhop website into the `web/` folder inside this new monorepo. Once it's done, we'll move on to extract the store and models we created in previous chapters to a new module called `@amazhop/logic`, and finally, we'll reimplement these models and the store through this package.

To get started with this section, we must start by cloning or copying the Amazhop website we implemented in previous chapters. To make things easier, you can just use this script:

```
cd packages/web/
npx degit "PacktPublishing/Redux-Made-Easy-with-Rematch/
packages/chapter-10"
```

This script will basically move our current directory to the web/ folder. Once we're in, we'll use the **degit** tool that we used in previous chapters to clone *Chapter 10, Rewrite a Full Code Base from JavaScript to TypeScript* code.

Now, we can move on to the logic/ folder where we're going to set up the Tsdx tool to help us with the bundling and testing of our logic. You'll remember this tool from *Chapter 9, Composable Plugins – Create Your First Plugin*:

```
cd ..
npx tsdx create logic --template basic
```

This will create practically all the code we need to make this module distributable, but let's adjust the package.json file a bit:

Let's install some development dependencies:

```
yarn add --dev msw redaxios @rematch/core @rematch/select @rema
tch/loading @rematch/immer redux
```

Change the package name to @amazhop/logic:

```
{
    "name": "@amazhop/logic"
}
```

Now, we must add to the peerDependencies property all the dependencies that the user should have installed in their website or application to bring this module in. Instead of shipping them, we just require them when this module is installed:

```
"peerDependencies": {
  "redaxios": ">=2",
  "@rematch/core": ">=2",
  "@rematch/select": ">=3",
  "@rematch/loading": ">=2",
  "@rematch/immer": ">=2",
  "redux": ">=4"
}
```

Now we can move the `store` folder and the `test` folder of our `web/` package into the `logic/` package. You can just execute this command from the root of the workspace:

```
cp -R packages/web/src/store packages/logic/src
cp -R packages/web/api packages/logic
cp -R packages/web/test/ packages/logic/test
rm -rf packages/logic/test/utils.tsx  && rm -rf packages/logic/
test/blah.test.ts
```

This will recursively copy all the `store` files and the `test` files that we used on the web to make sure that everything worked fine, and finally, run the `rm` command to delete unrequired files that shouldn't be copied.

Now, if you try to run `yarn test` inside the `@amazhop/logic` module, you will see that you need to adjust some typing or an incorrect path. Technically, if you make these changes, you should be able to run `yarn test` and see this:

```
yarn run v1.22.10
$ tsdx test
  PASS  src/models/cart.test.ts
  PASS  src/models/shop.test.ts


Test Suites: 2 passed, 2 total
Tests:       12 passed, 12 total
Snapshots:   1 passed, 1 total
Time:        2.091s
```

Basically, our test suite is passing correctly, as we expected initially, but there's still one interesting change. If we look at how we initialize the Rematch store, we should see something like this:

```
export const store = init<RootModel, FullModel>({
```

This is correct and works great, but how could we make the store a bit flexible for our needs, for example, by adding other plugins before the store initializes?

Right now, when `@amazhop/logic` is imported automatically, the store is initialized because it is just a constant executing the `init()` function. We could change this behavior by lazy loading the store. Just wrapping the `init()` function with a function will delay execution until we execute the function.

Let's change our `init()` function with a wrapped function that accepts a custom object with an `extraPlugins` property for adding plugins dynamically:

```
type LazyInitWithPlugins<R extends Models<R>, M extends
Models<R>> = {
  extraPlugins?: Array<Plugin<R, M>>
}
```

```
export const lazyStore = ({
  extraPlugins = []
}: LazyInitWithPlugins<RootModel, FullModel> = {}) =>
init<RootModel, FullModel>({
  models: { shop, cart },
```

This looks a bit messy, but there are just two generics, which are `RootModel` and `FullModel`, that could be changed if we add a plugin that needs to add some extra typing, and then we use arrow functions, `() =>`, to wrap our `init()` method and lazy load our store.

If we try to run `yarn test` now, we'll see that our test will fail because we need to execute the `store` method lazily because it's now a function and not a constant.

Thanks to TypeScript, we'll easily see what changes we need to make to render the testing suite operational again:

```
import { store, dispatch } from "../";    Module '"../"' has no exported member 'store'.

const getCart = () => store.getState().cart;
```

Figure 11.2 – TypeScript complaining about changes made to the store constant

Now, we export the `lazyStore` function, which needs to be executed lazily to recover the store. Before, we could just import the `store` constant and use it as shown in *Figure 11.2*.

Let's modify the previous errors to make the imports compatible with the `lazyStore` function:

```
import { lazyStore } from "../";
```

```
const store = lazyStore();
const { dispatch } = store;
const getCart = () => store.getState().cart;
```

With these changes applied, if we run `yarn test` again, we can check that everything runs fine.

It's also interesting to export some additional typing or functions that we'll need for our website or application on the `index.ts` file, such as the `filterByName` function:

```
export type Dispatch = RematchDispatch<RootModel>;
export type RootState = RematchRootState<RootModel, FullModel>;
export { filterByName, FullModel, RootModel }
```

As we did in *Chapter 9, Composable Plugins – Create Your First Plugin*, to build this package, we could use the `yarn build` script, which will generate UMD, CJS, and ESM builds for us, to be shipped through NPM with a simple `npm publish` command.

In the next section, we'll use this package in the Amazhop website using Yarn workspaces and lazy load our store accordingly. Also, we'll use the Rematch Persist plugin through the `extraPlugins` property.

Using the business logic in our Amazhop website

To get started with this section, we must add the `@amazhop/logic` package inside our `dependencies` list:

```
"dependencies": {
    "@amazhop/logic": "0.1.0",
```

Once it's done, just run `yarn install` to make sure that it's installed correctly.

And let's start with the first file on every Rematch implementation, initializing the store and wrapping our application with the Redux provider.

We could replace the whole `store/index.ts` file with just these 13 lines:

```
import { lazyStore, Dispatch, RootState } from "@amazhop/
logic";
import createPersistPlugin from "@rematch/persist";
import storage from "redux-persist/lib/storage";

export const store = lazyStore({
  extraPlugins: [
```

```
  createPersistPlugin({
    key: "cart-storage",
    storage,
    whitelist: ["cart", "shop"],
  }),
 ],
});
```

```
export const { dispatch } = store;
export type { Dispatch, RootState };
```

This file imports some utility types already filled with the `RootModel` and `FullModel` types from the `@amazhop/logic` package, and imports the `lazyModel` function we introduced previously. In this case, we're going to pass the `@rematch/persist` plugin since our website saves the `cart` and `shop` states before the user leaves the page. But in our React Native application, we don't want to persist any state, which is why we added the lazy initialization to be able to add custom configuration before the `init()` function runs.

Now, we can safely delete our `models/` folder, because the models are now inside the `@amazhop/logic` package and they're no longer required in our web package.

After deleting this folder, you will notice that the `filterByName` function on `src/components/ProductList/List` fails because it was exported from one model, but now we're exporting this function from the `@amazhop/logic` package, so you can safely change it to the following:

```
import { filterByName } from "@amazhop/logic";
```

Also, if the relative type imports to the `store` file are complex to you because of the relative dots, you could just use them directly from the `@amazhop/logic` package:

```
import type { RootState } from "../../store";
```

Just change relative paths to absolute imports using the `@amazhop/logic` package:

```
import type { RootState } from "@amazhop/logic";
```

If we run `yarn dev`, we should see everything runs smoothly and how it worked previously, but now our business logic is a distributable package that could be used anywhere, and at any time, with its own testing suite.

Also, as you'll remember, we integrated the `React Testing Library` package for testing our React components, and some of them are connected to this store, so if we run `yarn test`, we should see our testing suite turning green again.

This technique is a game-changer for many companies since it's common to build a website for our company product and end up building a mobile application or even another website with logic in common with the first one, and even with another framework, such as Vue. With Rematch, this scenario becomes easier than ever, maintainable, and predictable.

In the next section, we'll see how we can use this business logic inside a React Native application and how it will work out of the box without any complexity. Also, we'll look at some React Native concepts and styling utilities.

Creating a React Native application with Expo

To get started with this section, we're going to introduce a bit about what React Native is, what its main characteristics are, and what Expo tries to solve with React Native.

React Native is an open source mobile application framework created by Facebook, bringing React's declarative UI framework to iOS and Android, and also for Android TV, tvOS, and lately, even Windows and websites.

You might ask what's the main difference between React and React Native? Basically, they are virtually identical, but React Native doesn't manipulate the DOM via the virtual DOM as React does. It runs a background process that interprets the JavaScript used directly on the end device and uses a bridge to communicate with the native platform over this asynchronous bridge:

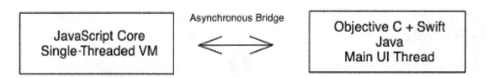

Figure 11.3 – React Native architecture

Instead of writing HTML elements, we must use React Native built-in components, or community ones, but never HTML or CSS. The reason is that these components are later replaced by native elements on each platform.

For example, the `View` component is the most fundamental component for building user interfaces with React Native. It is the container that supports layout, gesture handling, and accessibility controls.

We can write a `View` component like this:

```
import React from "react";
import { View, Text } from "react-native";

const ViewBoxText = () => {
  return (
    <View>
      <Text>Hello World!</Text>
    </View>
  );
};


export default ViewBoxText;
```

This code snippet creates a `View` component with a `Text` component inside it. When this code runs on Android, it will be replaced by `android.view`. If this code runs on iOS, it will be replaced by `UIView`, which is the native module that is used for this use case.

To style our components, we can use a prop named `style`, as React does. It accepts practically any CSS property.

For example, taking the previous code snippet, we could create a style for adding a `Text` component with a font size of `30` and the color `red`:

```
import { StyleSheet, View, Text } from "react-native";
...
<Text style={styles.h1}>Hello World!</Text>
...
const styles = StyleSheet.create({
  h1: {
    fontSize: 30,
    color: "red"
  }
})
```

With these concepts clear, we can move forward and look at why we are going to use Expo.

Expo (`https://expo.io`) is a framework for developing applications around React Native. Basically, we won't need to do practically anything to configure our project. Expo does the heavy lifting. We won't need Xcode or Android Studio software to deploy our application. This was impossible before Expo existed.

It also exports some custom components, navigation, and native features out of the box, such as **Push Notifications**, **Location services**, **Camera**, and **Social Authentication** – tons of features that, without Expo, are tedious to set up and even more so to publish for our end users.

Usually, to get started with Expo, we just need to run the amazing command-line interface that it offers:

```
expo init my-react-native-project
```

But, in our case, we're just going to clone the official template that we prepared for this chapter. Basically, it's the `expo init` result with all the dependencies we need to make it work, such as Rematch, Redux, and some development dependencies to make it easier to follow in this chapter.

As we did earlier in the book, let's use the **degit** tool to download the template on our machine. Make sure to be in the root of the monorepo working directory, since we'll download the template inside the `packages/app` folder:

```
npx degit "PacktPublishing/Redux-Made-Easy-with-Rematch#create-app-react-native" packages/app
```

This will download the template inside our monorepo. We should run `yarn install` to hoist all the packages, and when Yarn finishes installing our packages, we should move into the `app` module to run `yarn start`.

We should see this screen in our emulator – in this case, an iPhone 12 emulator:

Figure 11.4 – iPhone 12 emulator running the Amazhop application built with React Native and Expo

If you're able to see this screen, we're ready to move forward in this chapter and introduce our shared business logic, the @amazhop/logic package, and implement the React Native views for rendering the data.

Integrating the Amazhop logic

As we did in the web package, we have to add the `@amazhop/logic` package to the dependencies object of our `package.json` file and run `yarn install`:

```
"dependencies": {
    "@amazhop/logic": "0.1.0",
```

Now, we must wrap our React Native application with the Redux provider, as we did on the Amazhop website. Let's modify the `App.tsx` file:

```
import { Provider } from "react-redux";
import { lazyStore } from "@amazhop/logic";

export const store = lazyStore();
...
return (
    <SafeAreaProvider>
      <Provider store={store}>
        <Navigation />
        <StatusBar />
      </Provider>
    </SafeAreaProvider>
  )
}
```

Now, our application is correctly connected to the Rematch store so we can run `useDispatch` or `useSelector` hooks from any component that we use inside our application.

Let's navigate to the `screens/ShopScreen.tsx` file to add the required `useSelectors` hook and the `useDispatch` hook to dispatch some effects and reducers:

```
import { Dispatch, RootState, filterByName } from "@amazhop/
logic";
```

We import the `Dispatch` and `RootState` types from the `@amazhop/logic` package, and we also import the `filterByName` function, which we previously exported inside the `@amazhop/logic` package.

Now we're ready to integrate the selectors that will return the state that will use and dispatch the `getProducts()` effect:

```
const dispatch = useDispatch<Dispatch>();
const query = useSelector((rootState: RootState) => rootState.
shop.query);
const products = useSelector((rootState: RootState) =>
   query ? filterByName(rootState, query.toString()) :
   rootState.shop.products
);
const totalCartProducts = useSelector(
   (rootState: RootState) => rootState.cart.addedIds.length
);
const quantityById = useSelector(
   (rootState: RootState) => rootState.cart.quantityById
);

useEffect(() => {
   dispatch.shop.getProducts();
}, []);
```

This code snippet creates four constants:

- `query`: Returns the query value stored in our shop model
- `products`: Returns products filtered by name if the query is present, if not, it returns the shop products
- `totalCartProducts`: Returns the length of the `addedIds` property of our cart store
- `quantityById`: Returns the `quantityById` property from our cart store

Also, when the component is rendered for the first time, also called mounting will fire `getProducts()` effect, as you'll remember from the website implementation where we used the Intersection Observer API to know when to dispatch the `getProducts()` function. This API doesn't exist on React Native, but it offers an official solution for these use cases, called **FlatList**.

`FlatList` is a performant component for rendering lists in React Native, handles out-of-the-box horizontal mode, scroll loading, pull to refresh, and is, of course, cross-platform.

Let's use the previous constants and the products returned from our `getProducts()` effect to render an amazing view:

```
<View style={styles.container}>
  <View style={styles.topBar}>
    <Text style={styles.heading}>Amazhop</Text>
    <View>
      <TouchableOpacity onPress={() => navigation.
      navigate("Cart")}>
        <FontAwesome5 name="shopping-basket" size={24}
        color="#424242" />
      </TouchableOpacity>
      {totalCartProducts > 0 ? (
        <View style={styles.badge}>
          <Text style={styles.cartCount}>{totalCartProducts}</
          Text>
        </View>
      ) : null}
    </View>
  </View>
  <TextField value={query} />
  <FlatList
    data={products}
    numColumns={2}
    keyExtractor={(i) => i.id}
    onEndReached={() => dispatch.shop.getProducts()}
    onEndReachedThreshold={0.5}
    initialNumToRender={10}
    renderItem={({ item }) => (
      <View style={{ width: "50%" }}>
        <ProductCard data={item} quantity={quantityById[item.
        id] || 0} />
      </View>
    )}
  />
</View>
```

This code snippet is the whole view for our ShopScreen.tsx file, and as you can see, includes a TextField component for filtering products as we did in the website, and contains the FlatList component. Every time it reaches the bottom of the screen, it calls dispatch.shop.getProducts(), like we did with the Intersection Observer API, for creating an infinite scroll effect. It also contains a shopping basket icon that, when pressed, will navigate to the Cart screen.

We should see something like this in our emulator:

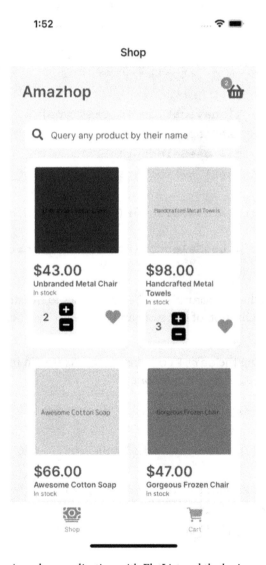

Figure 11.5 – The Amazhop application with FlatList and the logic correctly connected

So as not to make this chapter too long, the `ProductCard` component, which is the component that `FlatList` renders inside the list, is omitted. You can look at how the view is built in the official GitHub repository.

If you click on the heart icon, it will automatically mark or unmark the heart, as we did on the website. Also, you can decrease the quantity of the product added to the cart through the plus and minus buttons.

Now that we already have products added to the cart, we are going to modify `screens/CartScreen.tsx`. You'll remember from the Amazhop website that we built some selectors using `@rematch/select`, and for this view, they will be used too:

```
import { Dispatch, RootState } from "@amazhop/logic";
import { store } from "../App";
. . .
const CartScreen = ({ navigation }: CartType) => {
  const dispatch = useDispatch<Dispatch>();
  const quantityById = useSelector(
  (rootState: RootState) => rootState.cart.quantityById
  );
  const cartProducts = useSelector(store.select.cart.
  getCartProducts);
  const totalPrice = useSelector(store.select.cart.total);
. . .
```

We're using the selectors that `@rematch/select` exposes to the store correctly, even lazy loading the initialization of our store and even with TypeScript typings, and everything works fine.

Now, let's jump to rendering the `cartProducts` array. As we did in the `ShopScreen` list, we're going to use the `FlatList` component:

```
<View style={{ ...styles.container, minHeight: windowHeight }}>
  {cartProducts.length ? (
    <View style={{ maxHeight: windowHeight - 200 }}>
      <FlatList
        data={cartProducts as ProductType[]}
        keyExtractor={(i) => i.id}
        renderItem={({ item }) =>
          <View>
```

```
                    <CartCard
                        data={item}
                        quantity={quantityById[item.id] || 0}
                        key={item.id}
                    />
                </View>
            }
        />
```

This will render our `cartProducts` constant correctly. In this case, we don't use the `onEndReached` hook because we recover the whole cart once the screen is loaded.

To conclude this view, we can add a bottom footer for displaying the total cart and a button for restoring the cart when pressed, such as a `PLACE ORDER` button:

```
<View style={styles.totalContainer}>
    <Text style={styles.totalText}>Total</Text>
    <View style={styles.flex}>
        <Text style={styles.
        totalPriceText}>{number(totalPrice)}</Text>
    </View>
</View>
<Pressable
    onPress={() => {
        dispatch.cart.RESTORE_CART();
        navigation.navigate("Shop");
    }}
    style={styles.placeOrderTouchable}
>
    <Text style={styles.placeOrderText}>PLACE ORDER</Text>
</Pressable>
```

When clicking the **PLACE ORDER** button, the `RESTORE_CART` reducer will be executed and later the navigation will navigate us to the `ShopScreen` screen. In a real-world application, here, we'd probably include a Rematch effect that makes an asynchronous request to our backend for saving that order in our database, sending an email, or even both. Rematch makes these features easy since replacing an effect for a reducer or vice versa is as easy as using the global dispatch function with the corresponding effect or reducer name.

The result of our view should be something like this:

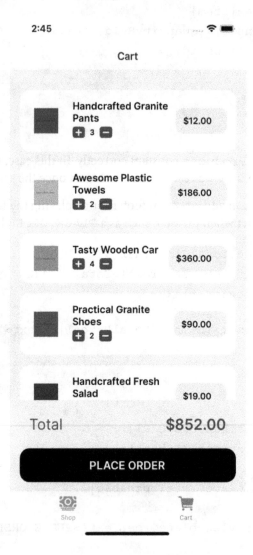

Figure 11.6 – The Amazhop application showing the Cart screen

We checked that running Rematch on any framework is as simple as using React Redux official hooks, some Rematch models, and in the case of using TypeScript, using the official Rematch utility types.

These steps will work for any framework out there if not using React with Redux. There are official and community bindings for integrating Redux and Rematch with ease.

In this section, we have learned a bit more about React Native and Expo. In summary, we demonstrated that using Rematch together with Redux and monorepo architectures improves the development experience and our flexibility to introduce new code and ship our products faster.

Summary

In this chapter, we have learned how to set up any Yarn workspace architecture and how it works internally. Also, we looked at React Native and Expo and how Rematch can ship totally framework-agnostic business logic that can be reused anywhere. Now you'll be able to create any monorepo architecture from scratch and ship framework-agnostic business logic with tools such as Tsdx and NPM. Also, you'll be able to create any React or React Native application or website using best practices and Rematch as the global state management solution.

In the next chapter, we'll analyze some of the most common performance optimizations we can apply to Rematch and React. We'll learn how to measure and, even better, how to prevent performance problems using the best techniques of caching, batching, and virtualizing.

12
Rematch Performance Improvements and Best Practices

In this chapter, we'll learn about how to apply performance improvements to our React and Rematch applications, and how these performance optimizations are commonly solved using memoization and common sense. We'll also learn what it means to virtualize and normalize data, and how we can measure our applications to see where our bottlenecks are located.

We'll learn about all these concepts through real examples, including the Amazhop website that we've built throughout the book. We'll also investigate which optimizations are appropriate for adding to our website and how we can track any performance issue on any website that we make with React.

In this chapter, we'll cover the following topics:

- Before optimizing, measure
- Debouncing and throttling
- Virtualizing large lists
- React optimizations
- Redux selectors with deep comparison
- Redux batching
- Data normalization

By the end of the chapter, you will be able to profile any website and discover what issues are causing bad performance. You will also be able to introduce performance improvements to any Rematch and React code base.

Technical requirements

To follow along with this chapter, you will need the following:

- Basic knowledge of **vanilla JavaScript** and the features of **ES6**
- Basic knowledge of **TypeScript**
- **Node.js >= 12**
- Basic knowledge of **React**
- A browser (**Chrome**, for instance)
- A code editor (**Visual Studio Code**, for instance)

You can find the code for this chapter in the book's GitHub repository at `https://github.com/PacktPublishing/Redux-Made-Easy-with-Rematch/tree/main/packages/chapter-12`.

Before optimizing, measure

Before jumping into this chapter, there's an idea that I would like to introduce: *If you can't measure it, you can't optimize it*. This seems straightforward enough, but sometimes we just forget this and focus on adding supposed performance optimizations where we probably don't need them, basically introducing technical debt where we shouldn't. Sometimes this technical debt becomes larger and larger and we lose control of our project as it becomes hard to maintain or, even worse, impossible to debug.

This might seem obvious, but sometimes it's not, and here we're going to learn how to measure – or at least learn about the main programs that we can use to benchmark – our application and see where it can be optimized.

Let's enumerate the three most important tools to track React performance issues and analyze how to fix them at runtime.

Google Chrome DevTools

Google Chrome DevTools is the window that every frontend programmer knows well because it's used for practically everything: examining the console, debugging our CSS, and even tracking which requests our website is dealing with and how. But these tools are more powerful than we could have ever imagined.

We can open the **Chrome DevTools** panel as usual, by right-clicking on our browser page and clicking **Inspect**. Then after accessing the **Performance** tab, we can use the record button, that is, the black solid circle at the top left of *Figure 12.1*.

This will capture web indicators such as **First Contentful Paint** (**FCP**) and the usage of our **Central Processing Unit** (**CPU**), and even take screenshots along a timeline, helping us to debug our website performance accordingly.

When we run this performance tool on the Amazhop website, we can see that almost all the indicators are green, meaning that we built a website that meets the best standards:

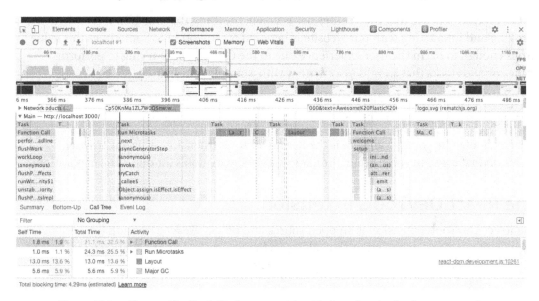

Figure 12.1 – Chrome DevTools Performance tab with Amazhop in development mode

There is tons of official documentation from Google on how to analyze the runtime performance of our websites using their tools, and so that's why I'm going to introduce one of the most important metrics that we should pay attention to when building a new website or improving an older one.

The first one is **Frames per Second** (**FPS**). Users are happiest when the animations on our website run at 60 FPS, and when this value drops lower than 24 FPS, the user experience will probably be negatively affected:

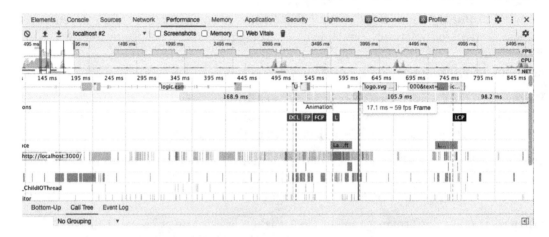

Figure 12.2 – The FPS indicator on the DevTools Performance tab

In our case, we can see that the **Frames** bar is green, meaning that our FPS value when scrolling and interacting with our website is between 50 and 60 FPS. Sometimes this value drops enough to harm the user experience due to the CPU or GPU trying to perform some complex tasks that should be rewritten with a simpler alternative.

Google Chrome DevTools offers a good solution to find out where and why our code is creating a bottleneck in our CPU/GPU and will help us to fix these issues.

The next tool we're going to analyze is the React DevTools extension. This is a browser extension that contains some useful profiling and debugging tools for our React applications.

The React DevTools extension

The React DevTools extension is an open source and official React extension for debugging our React applications that allows us to inspect the hierarchy of our React applications and profile where our components are re-rendered and why.

React DevTools works in a similar way to the Google Chrome DevTools **Performance** tab and contains a recording button where we can decide which interactions should be analyzed.

In this case, we're going to analyze the first render of our website. We can see that our **Flamegraph** is not bad at all. Since this is the first render, everything is slower than usual:

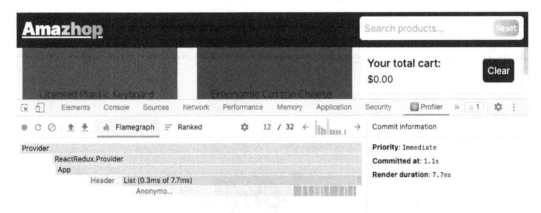

Figure 12.3 – React DevTools extension on the first load of Amazhop

Thanks to this extension and the profiling section, we discovered that when we reach the bottom and the **List** component requests more products, the whole list is re-rendered when it shouldn't be:

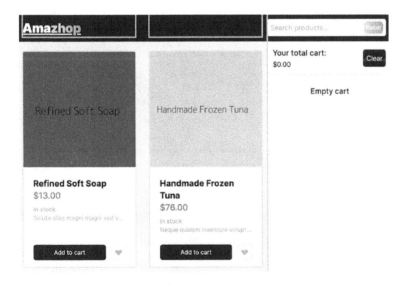

Figure 12.4 – Amazhop performance issue when fetching more data

This performance issue probably isn't noticeable on the first request, but what happens when it tries to re-paint 500 products in our infinite scroll? On modern devices, likely nothing happens, because they're powerful and React is fast, but imagine an Internet Explorer browser running on a machine with an old CPU – this behavior will make the FPS drop heavily and the page probably won't be usable.

We'll discover throughout this chapter how we can fix this situation with different alternatives.

Google Chrome Lighthouse

Google Chrome Lighthouse is also included under **Google Chrome DevTools**. It's an automated tool for improving the performance, quality, and correctness of our websites. Basically, under the hood, Lighthouse runs a battery of tests against the website and then generates a report on how well the website performed:

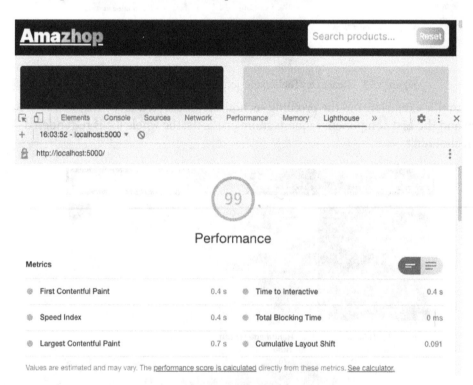

Figure 12.5 – Google Chrome Lighthouse score on Amazhop

In our case, our website performs extremely well when running the Lighthouse profiler, which suggests some options, including removing unused JavaScript files. Thanks to the Vite bundler and its tree-shaking technology, once this application is deployed to a production environment, the unused JavaScript files will automatically be removed.

In the next section, we'll discover some performance optimizations we can apply to our Amazhop website to improve the performance and FPS of our **List** component.

Debouncing and throttling

Debouncing and throttling techniques are used to limit the number of times a function can be executed.

For instance, with functions attached to events such as clicking on buttons, it is technically the user who decides when the function attached to the button executes and how many times. Sometimes this isn't good for the performance of our website, especially when our application is built with React and the performance is really tied to how many times the website re-renders.

With the debounce technique, it doesn't matter how many times the event is fired; it will be executed again only after the specified amount of time has passed after the user stops firing the event.

The most common usage for debouncing functions is adding an expensive callback when the user writes in the `<input />` element:

```
import debounce from "lodash.debounce";

export const InputElement = () => {
  const dispatch = useDispatch<Dispatch>();
  const [value, setValue] = useState("");

  useEffect(() => {
    dispatch.shop.SET_QUERY(value !== "" && value);
  }, [value]);

  return (
    <input
      onChange={(e) => setValue(e.target.value)}
      value={value}
      type="text"
      className="p-2 rounded-md w-full"
      placeholder="Search products..."
    />
  );
}
```

In this custom React component, we're basically using the `onChange` event to emit the `setValue` function, which is replacing the `value` state reference.

When the value state references change, it executes the `useEffect` life cycle, which is responsible for executing the `dispatch.shop.SET_QUERY` function with the new `value` state reference as a parameter.

It looks fine, but there is a problem: when the user writes one word, it works well, but what about when the user writes a long sentence? It will execute the function the same amount of times as the user's sentence length, because it is executed on every keypress, when it should just execute the function (for example, when the user stops writing after 300ms). This way, it will execute the `SET_QUERY` method just one time.

To introduce this, we just need to replace the `dispatch.shop.SET_QUERY` method with a debounced function of this method. We could create a native debounce function with `setTimeout` or use the `lodash` one instead:

```
import debounce from "lodash.debounce";

export const Header = () => {
  const dispatch = useDispatch<Dispatch>();
  const [value, setValue] = useState("");
  const debouncedDispatch = debounce(dispatch.shop.SET_QUERY,
  300);

  useEffect(() => {
    debouncedDispatch(value !== "" && value);
  }, [value]);
```

Instead of dispatching *N* times, the `debouncedDispatch` function will automatically execute only after the user stops writing and 300ms has passed. Debouncing usually solves a lot of performance issues in our web applications.

And what is throttling? What's the difference compared to debouncing? Basically, throttling executes the function at a regular interval, while debouncing will execute the function after some amount of time has passed since the last execution.

In the next section, we'll see some libraries that solve a pain point in the performance of our websites: rendering large lists, basically adding too many **Document Object Model** (**DOM**) nodes to our website.

Virtualizing large lists

List virtualization consists of just rendering items visible to the user. Essentially, when the user scrolls, we programmatically show the relevant items that should appear in the DOM and hide those that shouldn't.

Looking at our Amazhop website, you have probably noticed that we're rendering the whole `products` array even if a given product is not visible in the viewport. This is not an issue if we're rendering the first 10 products, but what about rendering 5,000 products, creating 5,000 nodes with 5,000 images when probably only 5 can be displayed? This makes no sense.

That's why some React folks created some libraries such as `react-window` and `react-virtual`, which reduce the amount of work and time required to render the initial page and, of course, for the process of updating this data.

In the next section, we'll see some React optimizations that we can include in our Amazhop application to avoid unnecessary re-renders and will also see how to discover these optimizations through browser tools such as Google Chrome DevTools and the React DevTools extension.

React optimizations

React, as you likely know, offers some functions for helping us in situations where our application is rendered more than desired. This feature is called **reconciliation**. When some component's props or state change, React re-renders and creates a thing called a virtual DOM, which is basically an object representation of our components that is used later to be compared against the actual DOM objects. If they're not equal, React will update the DOM.

The virtual DOM resides in React memory and performs all its operations on this rather than the actual browser DOM. This is because browser repaints are expensive tasks; React is smart enough to efficiently compare these object representations of our elements and decide when it should repaint our screen.

This is automatically done under the hood, but sometimes we have situations where we know that our components don't need to update. That's why React offers some life cycle events for classes, such as the following:

```
shouldComponentUpdate(nextProps, nextState) {
    return true;
}
```

`shouldComponentUpdate` is a life cycle event for React classes where we can decide when our component should reconcile. We can also use the `React.PureComponent` class, which is equivalent to implementing `shouldComponentUpdate()`, with a shallow comparison of the current and previous props and state.

Since we're not using classes on Amazhop, there's something similar for React functional components.

`React.memo()` is a **Higher-Order Component (HOC)** that basically checks for prop changes. This means that if our component is executed with the same props as the previous render, it will use the memoized one instead of re-rendering the component again.

Using the React DevTools extension, we can check that every time we reach the bottom, our previously rendered `Product` components are re-rendered because the parent component is rendered, but why should they re-render if their props are the same?

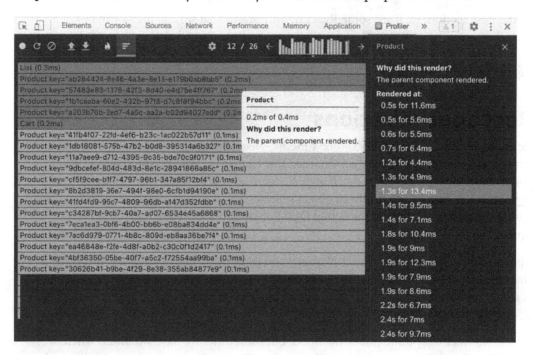

Figure 12.6 – React DevTools performance issue with product re-rendering

In this scenario `Product` components is re-rendered because the parent component is re-rendered, even when the Product props are the same, this is the perfect scenario for using `React.memo()` to fix this performance issue.

We just need to wrap our `Product` component with a memo HOC:

```
export const Product = React.memo(({ product }: ProductProps)
=> {
```

With just this change, our React application now automatically re-renders only the `Product` components that are new, or when the `product` prop changes.

React also offers two hooks for optimizing our React functional components, `useMemo` and `useCallback`.

useMemo

useMemo will only recompute the memoized value when one of the values inside the array, also called `deps`, has changed.

For example, taking the debounced function we introduced previously, we know that we can get a performance boost by memoizing the debounced function:

```
const debouncedDispatch = React.useMemo(
    () => debounce(dispatch.shop.SET_QUERY, 300),
    [dispatch]
);
```

Instead of recreating the debounced function every time the component re-renders, it is memoized and will only recompute when `dispatch` changes.

useCallback

Internally, both **useCallback** and `useMemo` use memoization. Basically, they remember something that happened in the past and they decide, given `deps`, whether they should forget the previous value and use the newest one, or return the older one like a cache.

The main difference of `useCallback` is that it remembers a function reference, while `useMemo` remembers the returned value of our function.

The following code snippet is essentially equivalent to the previous one implemented with `useMemo`:

```
const debouncedDispatch = React.useCallback(
    debounce(dispatch.shop.SET_QUERY, 300),
    [dispatch]
);
```

While `useCallback` memoizes functions, `useMemo` memoizes any computed value.

In the next section, we'll discover how Redux and Rematch can improve the performance of our application by avoiding unnecessary re-renders using shallow comparison.

Redux selectors with shallow comparison

You'll remember that the `useSelector` hook exported by the React Redux package introduces internal logic that only forces a re-render if the selector result appears to be different than the last result.

In version 7 of React Redux, a different result is determined by a strict reference comparison, using `===` under the hood to compare the new and previous values. If they're different, it will force a re-render.

That means if we return the same values in a different object reference, it will always re-render even if they're the same. Let's see this situation with a real example:

```
>  const or = { hi: 'hi' }
   const ar = { hi: 'hi' }
<  undefined
>  or === ar
<  false
>  shallowEqual(or, ar)
<  true
```

Figure 12.7 – Google Chrome console showing a strict reference comparison

Internally, what really matters to the `useSelector` hook to decide whether to re-render or not is the reference returned by the selector. It doesn't matter if other sections of the root state were updated; what matters is if the exact value returned by this selector changes, because the reference is the same.

This can be fixed in multiple ways, and you should choose the one you're most comfortable with.

Using the @rematch/select package

Basically, the `@rematch/select` package uses Reselect under the hood, which creates a memoized selector that returns multiple values in one object but only returns a new object when one of the values has changed.

The shallowEqual function

React Redux exports a function called `shallowEqual`, which performs a shallow equality comparison between the previous and new values to determine whether they are equivalent, as displayed in *Figure 12.7*. Using the `shallowEqual` function correctly determines whether the `or` and `ar` constants contain the same data even when their references aren't the same.

In the next section, we'll see how we can wrap multiple dispatch functions inside a unique re-render.

Redux batching

React Redux exports a function called `batch()`, which ensures that multiple actions dispatched outside of React only result in a single render update.

This works out of the box for Rematch and it's recommended in scenarios where our effects contain multiple dispatch executions to other models and we just need a single re-render update.

For example, imagine a Rematch effect that sets products to our state and then executes another effect that pushes some analytics to another model of our store:

```
dispatch.shop.SET_PRODUCTS({ products: data, totalCount });
dispatch.analytics.OTHER();
```

Since this logic is inside a Rematch effect, it doesn't run inside a React life cycle and will create two re-renders if we don't wrap this logic inside the `batch()` method:

```
import { batch } from "react-redux";
...
batch(() => {
  dispatch.shop.SET_PRODUCTS({ products: data, totalCount });
  dispatch.analytics.OTHER();
});
```

Just doing this will correctly render one single time instead of two.

As you will have noticed, most of the performance issues we encounter with React and Redux or Rematch are related to how many times our application re-renders and why. But sometimes there are some performance issues concerning the strategy we adopt when storing data inside Rematch/Redux stores. We usually end up storing too much data inside our stores, and even worse, we don't normalize this data, ending up with far too many duplications.

Data normalization

Some discussions appeared in the Rematch GitHub repository where some folks asked when and how they should save their data inside the store. We suggested the same thing as always: keep it simple.

If you need some local state that is not going to be used anywhere, use React's useState. If you need some local state that has side effects, you can use libraries that solve this, such as react-query, or even useEffect and useState together. And when you need to fetch some data or store some data that will be used in multiple screens, or you just want to fetch it once and use it anywhere, you can use Rematch with Redux, but always with data normalization.

Going back to the Amazhop application, as you'll remember, our cart state was something like this:

```
type CartState = {
  addedIds: Array<string>;
  quantityById: Record<string, number>;
};


const INITIAL_STATE: CartState = {
  addedIds: [],
  quantityById: {},
};
```

We created an addedIds array with the IDs stored as plain strings. quantityById is an object with IDs used as keys, and the values are the number of products added to the cart.

Technically, it would have been simpler to just create an array of products and store the whole product information inside the cart state, but we'll have that information duplicated because that product will be also stored inside the shop state – this is what we call data normalization.

We just need a copy of each piece of data in our state. Since it's a global state, we can access these values from anywhere, and we must, as much as we can, use arrays of IDs to store the keys and dictionaries to store the values. This leads to incredible performance when accessing these values and is highly maintainable.

After introducing all these performance improvements to any of our websites, we should probably notice nothing if we're using a modern browser and a modern computer, but we would probably notice a lot if we're using an older or lower-spec machine. These performance optimizations should only be introduced if we're sure that they're safe to add, as sometimes adding performance optimizations where we shouldn't causes errors that are hard to debug and track. That's why memoizing isn't the default behavior for components, stores, or selectors.

Summary

In this chapter, we have learned how to easily profile any React application and have seen how Google Chrome DevTools can help us to debug and track performance issues with our websites. We also learned some best practices, including virtualizing large lists and normalizing data, to improve the performance of our websites, and we have seen some React optimizations that we can start using in our projects.

The next chapter is the last one, and we'll finish with some personal conclusions about how Rematch will iterate over the future with other state management solutions that have appeared lately, along with how Rematch and Redux will co-exist with these new state management tools.

13
Conclusion

This chapter is the concluding chapter of this book. We're going to talk briefly about what we have learned throughout the book, and how we tried to teach Rematch with real-world situations, including a complete shopping store and a React Native application. The future is moving fast, and in this chapter, we'll try to unravel what the next steps are that state management libraries are trying to solve and how they're reinventing themselves, even Redux.

In this chapter, we'll cover the following topics:

- Wrapping up
- The future of Rematch
- The future of Redux
- Curtains down

By the end of the chapter, you will understand the actual position of Rematch in state management libraries and the alternative state management solutions that have appeared during 2020 and 2021.

Wrapping up

Reaching the end of the book brings us joy, especially because this book was about Rematch but ended up being a small roadmap that every frontend developer should take, starting from the foundations and learning why Redux was created, and what problem it tried to solve – and we kept that methodology throughout every chapter, asking what the problem was and how we could fix that problem. This was broken into three parts, as follows.

Rematch essentials

From *Chapter 1, Why Redux? An Introduction to Redux Architecture*, to *Chapter 4, From Redux to Rematch – Migrating a To-Do App to Rematch*, we focused on understanding why and how Redux was created, looking at the motivations that led to the creation of Rematch. We also started to work with some code, creating a vanilla JavaScript website using Redux and then migrating it to Rematch.

Building real-world websites with Rematch

From *Chapter 5, React with Rematch – The Best Couple – Part I*, to *Chapter 8, The Rematch Plugins Ecosystem,* we created an amazing shopping website from the ground up using React and Tailwind for the styling. For the bundling system, we learned what Vite is and examined the differences between Vite and other common bundlers, such as webpack and Rollup.

Also, we introduced side-effects into Rematch for the first time, making API calls to a fake server that returned products for our shop, and we created an infinite scroll system where the user doesn't need to load a new page to fetch more products.

All these features were completely tested with Jest and the React Testing Library. We introduced 98% testing coverage in our project, which gave us the confidence to refactor the whole code base to TypeScript in the next part.

And to conclude with this part, we introduced and explained in depth which Rematch plugins are official, how they work internally, and how they can solve the pain points of Redux with a minimal footprint.

Diving deeper into Rematch

From *Chapter 9, Composable Plugins – Create Your First Plugin*, to *Chapter 12, Rematch Performance Improvements and Best Practices,* we dived into more complex scenarios such as creating a Rematch plugin from scratch, following the official recommendations, such as using the Tsdx module to bundle and test the plugin. We used the plugin internally in our Amazhop website.

Also, we completely migrated our Amazhop website and our testing suite to TypeScript, and we analyzed in depth how Rematch TypeScript utility types make it a pleasure to work with TypeScript and our Rematch models.

All the logic we implemented in the book to build the Amazhop website gave us an amazing background to start developing new applications with Rematch, since we learned how to extract this logic to distributable packages using Tsdx, and also we learned how monorepo architectures work. We also ended up using the same logic for the website and for a completely new React Native with Expo application.

To conclude, we talked about some performance optimizations we can include in every Rematch or Redux application, and how React exports some utility functions to make memoization easier.

All this code has been completely published and separated by chapters in the official GitHub repository of this book. It contains a monorepo architecture using Yarn workspaces and includes a continuous integration function where, on every push, the whole repository installs the dependencies and runs ESLint, Jest, and TypeScript tests for every module. In this way, we'll keep the repository updated for any dependency changes:

`https://github.com/PacktPublishing/Redux-Made-Easy-with-Rematch`

The future of Rematch

Rematch's future will see the whole repository being updated as much as possible. Every 3-6 months we create an iteration plan where we, along with the community, define the next roadmap for Rematch. Everything is discussed with the community and we keep working hard to be one of the best state-management solutions out there, with a minimal footprint for our bundle size and an incredible development experience.

We continue working hard on the documentation side, where we recently introduced a rewrite of the website (`https://rematchjs.org`) to offer an amazing experience in terms of performance and content.

Also, we keep the focus on TypeScript compatibility, where we have set up a GitHub Action that every night runs the whole Rematch testing suite, which runs more than 200 integration tests and unit tests against the TypeScript nightly version. TypeScript nightly versions are versions of TypeScript that are published every night to NPM with the actual code of the main branch of TypeScript. This means that before TypeScript releases a new version, we have already tested that Rematch works fine with it.

We'll continue providing compatibility with future versions of Redux and React Redux and we hope you find Rematch useful enough to use it in your projects.

The future of Redux

Redux has changed a lot in the last 2 years, since a new package appeared in its scope, called **Redux Toolkit**, that basically tries to solve the same problems that Rematch solved a while ago:

- Configuring the Redux store when using non-standard scenarios is complicated.
- Creating complex applications that handle side-effects requires installing too many packages that are not official or officially supported by the Redux team.
- Redux needs too much boilerplate code.

Redux Toolkit is intended to be the standard way to write Redux logic creation. Since it was heavily inspired by solutions such as Rematch, it aims to create an official solution for the problem of maintainability we spoke about in this book.

Should we use Redux Toolkit instead of Rematch? Probably, or maybe not. You're free to use whatever you want; you should always choose whatever fits your requirements.

Redux Toolkit is an official solution with more visibility and contributors, and in the future, probably all web applications built with Redux will use Redux Toolkit, but there are some things that in my honest opinion Rematch does better.

Rematch is considered by some people to be a framework because of its extendibility, but it's not – it is less than 2 KB in size and is just an abstraction layer that you could build on your own side, but adding the Rematch Plugins section adds a whole ecosystem of reusable and pluggable logic, including `@rematch/loading`, `@rematch/immer`, and `@rematch/select`.

Rematch is fully compatible with TypeScript and makes migrating old-style Redux code bases pretty straightforward. Also, Redux Toolkit is compatible out of the box with TypeScript and, given the use case, could be easier to set up than Rematch.

However, there are still some scenarios such as side-effects where Redux Toolkit still uses the Redux Thunk strategy using `createAsyncThunk`. It also works with `async/await` syntax. The main difference between Redux Toolkit and Rematch is that Rematch lets you define thunk-like logic in the `effects` property of the Rematch models, keeping the logic a bit more encapsulated.

I highly recommend looking at the Redux Toolkit documentation at `https://redux-toolkit.js.org` and giving it a try – create some projects with Redux Toolkit and Rematch and take the one that fits your needs better.

Curtains down

I would like to give a huge thanks to Shawn McKay and Blair Bodnar for creating this amazing library some years ago and trusting me to take on the role of leading the whole rewriting of the library and maintaining it until today.

Thanks to all the contributors that contributed to making Rematch what it is today – this book is thanks to all of you.

And thank you, reader, for taking the time to read this book and for your interest in Rematch development.

`Packt.com`

Subscribe to our online digital library for full access to over 7,000 books and videos, as well as industry leading tools to help you plan your personal development and advance your career. For more information, please visit our website.

Why subscribe?

- Spend less time learning and more time coding with practical eBooks and Videos from over 4,000 industry professionals

- Improve your learning with Skill Plans built especially for you

- Get a free eBook or video every month

- Fully searchable for easy access to vital information

- Copy and paste, print, and bookmark content

Did you know that Packt offers eBook versions of every book published, with PDF and ePub files available? You can upgrade to the eBook version at `packt.com` and as a print book customer, you are entitled to a discount on the eBook copy. Get in touch with us at `customercare@packtpub.com` for more details.

At `www.packt.com`, you can also read a collection of free technical articles, sign up for a range of free newsletters, and receive exclusive discounts and offers on Packt books and eBooks.

Other Books You May Enjoy

If you enjoyed this book, you may be interested in these other books by Packt:

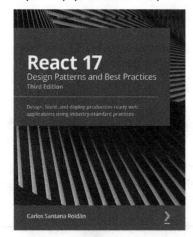

React 17 Design Patterns and Best Practices - Third Edition

Carlos Santana Roldán

ISBN: 978-1-80056-044-4

- Get to grips with the techniques of styling and optimizing React components
- Create components using the new React Hooks
- Get to grips with the new React Suspense technique and using GraphQL in your projects
- Use server-side rendering to make applications load faster
- Write a comprehensive set of tests to create robust and maintainable code

Full-Stack React, TypeScript, and Node

David Choi

ISBN: 978-1-83921-993-1

- Discover TypeScript's most important features and how they can be used to improve code quality and maintainability
- Understand what React Hooks are and how to build React apps using them
- Implement state management for your React app using Redux
- Set up an Express project with TypeScript and GraphQL from scratch
- Build a fully functional online forum app using React and GraphQL
- Add authentication to your web app using Redis
- Save and retrieve data from a Postgres database using TypeORM

Packt is searching for authors like you

If you're interested in becoming an author for Packt, please visit authors.
packtpub.com and apply today. We have worked with thousands of developers and
tech professionals, just like you, to help them share their insight with the global tech
community. You can make a general application, apply for a specific hot topic that we are
recruiting an author for, or submit your own idea.

Hi!

I Sergio Moreno, author of *Redux Made Easy with Rematch*. I really hope you enjoyed reading this book and found it useful for increasing your productivity and efficiency in Redux with Rematch.

Hope this book gave you enough confidence to be able to create any website or application that comes to your mind, we're extremely lucky of being programmers.

It would really help me (and other potential readers!) if you could leave a review on Amazon sharing your thoughts on *Redux Made Easy with Rematch*.

Go to the link below or scan the QR code to leave your review:

https://packt.link/r/1801076219

Your review will help me to understand what's worked well in this book, and what could be improved upon for future editions, so it really is appreciated.

Best wishes,

Index

S

W

workspaces
  about 213
  creating 215
  setting up 214, 215

Y

yarn
  using, to install
    react-infinite-scroll-hook 105
Yarn 62
yarn build command 117
Yarn workspaces
  architecture 213

Z

Zombie Notifications 6